What if you had the tools to live an abundant life and overcome the lies of the enemy? The sixty devotionals in Carolyn Dale Newell's *Faith that Walks on Water* hands you the right tools to break free from fear, worry, and stress and walk into a bold new faith.

Linda Evans Shepherd
Ministry leader and author

In her sixty-day devotional, *Faith that Walks on Water*, Carolyn takes you on a journey to a deeper faith built on the true character of God. Carolyn's blindness gives her unique insight into what it means to walk by faith and not by sight—and her gift, as she calls her blindness, is our gift in this book. Walk alongside Carolyn for sixty days and allow God to strengthen your faith as you learn to trust Him more. You don't want to miss this book.

Mary R. Snyder
Speaker

Carolyn Dale Newell is a remarkable woman of God. In *Faith that Walks on Water*, you'll get sixty devotionals and journal prompts to turn fear into rock-solid faith. Each entry will captivate your mind with a biblical truth, give you an opportunity to ponder the key scriptural concept, and then guide you to journal in response to what God reveals to your heart. If you're looking for a devotional that will help you to grow in your walk with God, this is it!

Carol Kent
Author of *He Holds My Hand: Experiencing God's Presence and Protection*

Faith that Walks on Water offers a fresh voice addressing issues we all face. Carolyn Dale Newell's deep love for God's Word is evidenced in each of the devotional entries. She walks with her readers through the process of learning to implement truth combined with the love of God for the purpose of transformation. This book speaks life, and I can't wait for the ladies of my church to take the journey with Carolyn as she helps them build faith that can walk on water.

Sheri Hawley
Pastor, Garden Grove Church in Winter Haven, FL

As I've journeyed through a difficult trial in recent years, I've learned from my daily time with Jesus that He is near to our broken hearts and enables us to carry joy and sorrow in the same hand. Carolyn's devotional reiterates this message in a vulnerable and authentic way. Every day you will be encouraged to ponder and put into practice meaningful spiritual application and experience the mighty hand of God when you step out in faith on the wavy seas.

Christine Trimpe
Author of *Seeking Joy through the Gospel of Luke:
A Christmas to Calvary Advent Countdown*

FAITH
THAT
Walks
ON
WATER

CAROLYN DALE NEWELL

FAITH THAT *Walks* ON WATER

Conquering Emotional Bondage with the Armor of God

REDEMPTION PRESS

Published by Redemption Press, PO Box 427, Enumclaw, WA 98022.
Toll-Free (844) 2REDEEM (273-3336)

Redemption Press is honored to present this title in partnership with the author. The views expressed or implied in this work are those of the author. Redemption Press provides our imprint seal representing design excellence, creative content, and high-quality production.

The author has tried to recreate events, locales, and conversations from memories of them. In order to maintain their anonymity, in some instances the names of individuals, some identifying characteristics, and some details may have been changed, such as physical properties, occupations, and places of residence.

Unless otherwise indicated, all Scripture quotations are from the New King James Version®. Copyright © 1982 by Thomas Nelson. Used by permission. All rights reserved.

Scripture quotations marked (NIV) are from the Holy Bible, New International Version®, NIV®. Copyright © 1973, 1978, 1984, 2011 by Biblica, Inc.™ Used by permission of Zondervan. All rights reserved worldwide. www.zondervan.com The "NIV" and "New International Version" are trademarks registered in the United States Patent and Trademark Office by Biblica, Inc.™

Scripture quotations marked (NLT) are from the Holy Bible, New Living Translation, copyright ©1996, 2004, 2015 by Tyndale House Foundation. Used by permission of Tyndale House Publishers, Carol Stream, Illinois 60188. All rights reserved.

ISBN 13: 978-1-64645-614-7 (Paperback)
978-1-64645-613-0 (ePub)
978-1-64645-612-3 (Mobi)

Library of Congress Catalog Card Number: 2022915994

Contents

INTRODUCTION

DO YOU REALIZE A BATTLE RAGES IN YOUR MIND? DAILY BATTLES. Hourly battles, and when you lose just one battle, your heart aches as the floor beneath you trembles. Then you awake to fight the same battles all over again.

You've endured heart-wrenching trials. Perhaps stormy waves surround you now. The cancer trial, the wayward child, the depression, the vision loss. I mark those trials with a Roman numeral in the outline of my life. But tucked away in each of those traumatic seasons, the smaller battles occurred: the fear that haunted me like an old, abandoned house full of cobwebs, the worry that forbade my mind to rest, and the rejection that labeled me as unacceptable. Shame followed me around like a long-lost childhood friend. Bitterness made forgiving feel incredibly impossible, and I still try to conquer stress today.

These emotions plus a healthy dose of discouragement and a side order of despair plague us regularly. For most of my Christian life, I never realized Satan held me in emotional bondage. Nobody told me that Jesus's victory on the cross gave me more than victory over sin. I didn't realize the abundant life began on earth, and I don't have to wait until I reach the pearly gates to enjoy it.

For the past six years, my mission has been to win the victory over negativity and emotions while equipping women just like you to live a victorious, abundant life. No more rides on the emotional roller coaster.

I'm glad you chose this book, ready to embark on a journey to a faith you once thought possible only for the super spiritual. Are

11

you ready for a life-transforming adventure? Many books make that promise, but with a devotional journal, you will mark your progress as we move forward.

Sweet friend, I have prayed for you through every aspect of writing this book. I've prayed for God to make a way when it seems impossible. I've prayed for God to transform both of us, because I am still a work in progress myself, and I'll continue to pray as you read.

If you're ready to start bossing your emotions around instead of your emotions being the boss of you, let's set sail. We'll travel to the deep seas, put the anchor down, and then, hand in hand, we'll walk on water.

The night Jesus came walking on the water to His disciples, He strolled over churning waves. What had frightened these seasoned fishermen? A violent storm on the Sea of Galilee. Jesus came to help His disciples while walking over the stormy waters. My friend, we can walk all over our storms too.

Once you finish this book, you can look back and see just how far Jesus has brought you. And on those tough days, keep this book handy and turn to the section for the specific emotion threatening you that day. It's here in case of an emergency.

Imagine a life virtually void of negativity, fear, and shame. The feelings of rejection will fade into a memory. Typical stressful days won't be so bumpy. Even the pangs of depression and grief will be a bit more tolerable.

I'm ready to set sail when you are. All you have to do is turn the page.

PART I

Faith 101

DAY 1

Why Should I Climb Out of the Boat?

The thief does not come except to steal, and to kill, and to destroy. I have come that they may have life, and that they may have it more abundantly.

John 10:10

STEPPING OUT OF THE BOAT FOR ME MEANT STEPPING OUTSIDE MY front door. I missed my peaceful walks by the woods listening to birds sing and longed to return to my joy-filled excursions. But first, I would have to grip the doorknob and step outside. I'd have to walk with my white cane and pray I'd never get lost again.

Stepping out of the boat makes incredible life changes possible. It's where we see promises fulfilled and victories won. It makes heroes out of ordinary people.

But stepping out of the boat isn't for everyone. Out of twelve disciples, only Peter asked to walk on water. About two million Israelites marched out of Egypt, but only Joshua and Caleb crossed into the promised land. Only Elijah stood for God against four hundred prophets of Baal. David volunteered to fight Goliath while the entire Israelite army trembled in their armor.

What's wrong with sitting in the boat? Absolutely nothing. We cling to the security of the boat, so why should we climb out?

Something amazing awaits us out on the open sea. Jesus stands there with His nail-scarred hand outstretched toward us. We will experience Him in extraordinary ways never before possible. Our faith will soar. The unknown won't seem so frightening. Stress won't weigh us down. Rejection won't hold us hostage. The abundant life Jesus promises begins when we take that first step.

The Greek word translated as *abundant* means superior. The New Living Translation (NLT) translates it as "rich and satisfying." The Amplified Bible reads "to the full, till it overflows."

It's okay to stay in the boat, but when we make that choice, some blessings will slip right through our fingers. If I hadn't stepped out onto the waves, I wouldn't have moved from a white cane to my beautiful black Lab, Iva, and hours of laughter. Even more, I would have missed out on the independence I gained as a blind woman led by a guide dog.

It takes more faith to climb out of the boat than it does to walk on water.

Will you join me? Will you trust Jesus like Peter did? I'm extending my hand to you. Let's step out together.

Ponder and Practice

In Numbers chapters 13 and 14, Moses sent twelve spies, including Joshua and Caleb, into Canaan to bring them a report about the land. Two men returned carrying a cluster of grapes between them (Numbers 13:23). Read Numbers 13:27–33. Joshua isn't mentioned, but he shared the same beliefs as Caleb. They trusted God to deliver them.

What observations can you make about Caleb from these verses? In what ways are you like Joshua and Caleb? Would you be more likely to speak out like Caleb or obey quietly like Joshua?

Read Numbers 14:1–12. Why did God become angry with Israel? If you had been an Israelite, how do you think you would have responded and why?

_____

_____

_____

Now read Numbers 14:22–24. What promises did God make to Caleb?

_____

_____

_____

What correlation do you see between entering Canaan with its giants and stepping out of the boat?

_____

_____

_____

Prayer

Lord, it took faith to cross into the promised land. I need that same bold faith. Grab my hand as I step out of the boat. Amen.

DAY 2

What If I Sink?

But when he saw that the wind was boisterous, he was afraid;
and beginning to sink he cried out, saying, "Lord, save me!"
Matthew 14:30

I DIDN'T EVEN KNOW HOW TO SPELL LEUKEMIA, BUT IT SOON
became part of our daily conversation. Newlyweds usually focus on
choosing who gets which side of the closet. Instead, we battled for my
husband Timmy's life through those foundational years.

During that tear-filled season, I needed to trust God wholeheart-
edly, but I couldn't pry my fingers from the side of the boat. What if
God allowed my husband to die?

At least Peter stepped out of the boat before his eyes moved off
Jesus and onto the waves. I couldn't peel my eyes off the waves threatening to sink me. As a young Christian, I hadn't grasped God's love
and sovereignty. I feared sinking, so I clung to the boat.

Peter took that first step of faith. In the presence of Jesus on the
churning waves, Peter's faith increased until he focused on the waves
of doubt. "Save me!" Immediately, Jesus rescued Peter.

Sinking isn't deadly. It isn't even dangerous. Friend, when we cry
out, Jesus will save us, just like He rescued Peter.

Moments of sinking become moments for strengthening.

I didn't walk on water during Timmy's cancer, but I discovered
the riches of God's faithfulness. In just two days, Timmy and I will

celebrate twenty-three years of marriage. My microscopic faith blossomed in the fertile soil of grace. God showered us with miracles, small and large. I learned to trust God, and I became strong enough to step out in faith during the next storm.

The fear of sinking prevents us from living the abundant life. Are you sailing through stormy waters today? Are you ready to take that first step, or are you clinging to the side? Do you trust Jesus to save you if you begin to sink?

Ponder and Practice

Reflect on the storms you have weathered. On a separate sheet of paper or on the notes app of your phone, write down all your moments of sinking.

Go through your list and write down how God strengthened you during those moments of sinking.

What patterns of growth do you see?

If you are navigating a storm now, what doubts prevent you from focusing on Jesus's truth? I wish I could be with you today, but I am saying a special prayer for you right now.

_____

_____

_____

Doubts come from our enemy and often begin with *what if* or *how could God*. We wear the belt of truth (Ephesians 6:12). Replace each doubt you face with the truth in God's Word to replace the lie. Here's an example:

My doubt: What if Timmy dies?
God's truth: "And we know that all things work together for good to those who love God, to those who are the called according to His purpose" (Romans 8:28).

_____

_____

_____

Prayer

Lord Jesus, You are the truth, and the truth will set us free from all the doubts and lies of the enemy. Reveal Your truth to me today. I trust You in my moments of sinking because You will never allow me to drown. In Jesus's name. Amen.

DAY 3

What's the Difference between Faith and Believing?

*Now faith is the substance of things hoped
for, the evidence of things not seen.*

Hebrews 11:1

I FELT IVA'S HEAD GENTLY MOVING FROM SIDE TO SIDE. WAS SHE watching the traffic on the busy street ahead as we approached it? The bright sun allowed me enough light to watch her follow the traffic. Suddenly, a car slowed down, and Iva pulled me to the left curb. The car whipped into our street.

The first time that happened, I grasped a new understanding of faith. As I walk by faith, Iva walks by sight. God guides me by His sight as I walk by faith in Him.

During a Bible study, I realized faith moves in accordance with our beliefs. Faith isn't what we believe. It's how we act. That's why the Bible calls it walking by faith.

When our beliefs line up with the truth of God, they provide us with a sound foundation for our faith. We don't base our faith on what we see, hear, smell, touch, or taste. That's walking by sight. Our faith rests in God alone. As today's verse states, our faith relies on the evidence of God's Word and His faithfulness. Then we begin living out what we believe.

Faith is the progress by which we walk out the beliefs we process.

We believe we can do all things through Christ (Philippians 4:13). We walk out our faith by not cowering in fear, because we trust God to equip us. We believe God provides our needs (Philippians 4:19). We refuse worried thoughts when we trust God's provision.

We believe the truth of Scripture. We can talk about our beliefs. We can only demonstrate our faith by the way we live. It's not in our talk but in our walk.

As my sight faded, I found that walking without sight physically taught me how to walk by faith spiritually. Physically, I trust Iva, my cane, and my skills. Thankfully, I can walk by spiritual faith because my trust rests in God Almighty. Who we place our faith in outweighs the size of our faith. That's why we need only a mustard seed-sized faith.

Are you walking by faith? It's all right if you're not, because beginning today, you will discover how to live a faith-filled life. Learning the difference between our beliefs and faith helps us understand the foundational truths of real faith.

Ponder and Practice

"Faith is acting like it's so even when it's not so, in order that it might be so simply because God said so."[1] Dr. Tony Evans used these words to explain faith. In your own words, explain the difference between faith and belief.

_____

_____

_____

What is one of your favorite promises from the Bible?

_____

_____

How does this promise encourage you?

_____

_____

_____

What changes can you make this week to walk this promise out by faith?

_____

_____

_____

"Therefore I say to you, whatever things you ask when you pray, believe that you receive them, and you will have them" (Mark 11:24). Does any disbelief prevent you from believing this promise? Ask God to show you how to overcome your doubt and to help you believe.

_____

_____

_____

Have you ever believed God in the face of doubt? How were those beliefs attacked, and how did you walk out your faith?

_____

_____

_____

Prayer

Lord Jesus, forgive me for doubting. This faith thing is difficult to grasp, but You are faithful. Lord, help my unbelief! Amen.

DAY 4

Walking in Victory

For the message of the cross is foolishness to those who are perishing, but to us who are being saved it is the power of God.

1 Corinthians 1:18

I HAVE A SECRET THE DEVIL DOESN'T WANT YOU TO KNOW, AND sometimes I forget it myself. When we traversed the 2020 COVID lockdowns, I wanted my speaking schedule back. I wanted my church opened, and so did you. I stomped around like a toddler unable to have my way.

I began living in defeat, a place we visit often. Sometimes, we camp out there. Defeated by depression, defeated by fear, defeated by unforgiveness, defeated by comparison, or defeated by stress. Take your pick.

By now, your mind has traveled to a season when you felt trapped by something beyond your control. Perhaps you carry that overwhelming weight now.

Here's the secret: We don't have to live in defeat because Christ conquered it on the cross. Christ didn't die just to give us eternal life. He died to give us abundant life, and that excludes defeat. Each hopeless moment was nailed to the cross, and we have victory.

Why do we still struggle with defeat? When the enemy begins oppressing us, we choose worldly wisdom over God's wisdom.

Our verse says we are being saved. Jesus delivered us from hell, but daily He delivers us from the effects of sin.

In his commentary, Dr. Tony Evans explains that we access the power of Christ through the cross. But like the Corinthians, we short-circuit that available power when we don't plug into it for daily needs.[2] We don't want to bother God with that nagging worry, so instead of praying, we don't plug in and we walk in defeat.

Instead of continuing to live by worldly wisdom when fear strikes, when stress accelerates, or when discouragement overwhelms, let's turn to the cross.

The Greek word translated here as *power*, according to *Strong's Concordance*, connotes a miraculous force—and I need that daily.[3] Sweet friend, I've given up on the world's ways of handling my emotions. Pretending they don't exist and stuffing them down never works. I want victory! What about you?

I don't live in defeat because Christ has already given me the victory.

Are you ready to deny the foolishness of the world and turn to the power of the cross for everything? Making God's wisdom your sole perspective will feel natural once you make the switch.

Ponder and Practice

Read Colossians 2:14–15. When the Romans crucified someone, they nailed a list of their crimes to the cross. That's why "King of the Jews" was nailed to Jesus's cross. At His crucifixion, all our sins were nailed there. While everyone mourned the death of Jesus, His Spirit declared victory over Satan and his demons when He disarmed them.

Likewise, all our troublesome emotions and negative thoughts have been conquered on the cross. List negative thoughts and emotions you currently struggle with. We'll refer back to the list in the future. Take your time and include as many as possible.

_____

_____

_____

_____

_____

Prayer

Lord, bring to mind everything I need to leave at the cross today. Give me the strength to walk forward in victory. Shine Your wisdom on my life, because what I've been doing isn't always working. In Jesus's name. Amen.

DAY 5

Are You Having a Crucifixion Today?

For those who live according to the flesh set their minds
on the things of the flesh, but those who live accord-
ing to the Spirit, the things of the Spirit.

Romans 8:5

WHO SITS ON THE THRONE OF YOUR LIFE, YOU OR THE HOLY SPIRIT?
This morning, my flesh fought to overthrow the Spirit from the throne.
Overnight, our refrigerator stopped running. Everything felt warm.
My mind raced to all the shortages. Will the repair technician have
the part on their truck? Will we have to wait days or possibly weeks to
have a working refrigerator? And having a new one delivered would
take over two months now.

How ironic that an internal battle raged on the day I planned to
write this devotional. When I prayed and praised God through several
of the psalms, peace reigned, and yes, the part was on the truck!

The world depletes us daily with home repairs, car repairs, and
various struggles. Problems at work and in the world discourage us.
For us to live a Spirit-filled life, we must crucify the flesh daily and
fill up on the Spirit.

Today's verse says we must set our minds on the Spirit in order
to live by the Spirit. That means we have to clear our minds of all
fleshly thoughts, like the panic I experienced earlier. Our minds must

be saturated with spiritual things. This goes beyond our thoughts to our attitudes.

A Holy Spirit–controlled life will not depend on self. Counselors from the Department for the Blind urged me to live a successful independent life. I have found that when I get self-reliant, I will fail because I left God out.

When God saved us, His Holy Spirit came to live within us. When we allow Him to dominate our lives, we walk in the Spirit. He is our helper. We aren't doing this alone. But if we still allow flesh to rule, we will never live the abundant life.

Turmoil occurs when I am flesh driven and not Spirit led.

To grow spiritually, we must give the Spirit full rein. That includes every aspect of life. We cannot say, *Holy Spirit, I give You everything but my money.*

We have to put the members of the flesh to death daily. Then we can ask the Holy Spirit to refuel us for this day.

Ponder and Practice

One of my favorite verses I use to direct my thoughts is found in Colossians: "Set your mind on things above, not on things on the earth" (Colossians 3:2).

List three earthbound thoughts on your mind today. Beside each one, list a heavenly thought to replace it.

_____

_____

_____

What areas do you need to release to the Holy Spirit today? Begin praying over them as you relinquish them to the Lord.

_____

_____

_____

Read Galatians 5:16–26. According to verse 16, how do we keep from gratifying, or fulfilling, the desires of the flesh?

_____

_____

_____

Another deterrent to walking in the Spirit is sin. Yes, we all mess up daily, but when we willfully sin, Paul says we live by the flesh (Galatians 5:19–21). Sin grieves the Holy Spirit, requiring us to crucify our flesh.

Rewrite verse 24 in your own words.

_____

_____

_____

Prayer

Holy Spirit, I welcome You. Show me how I have grieved You and quenched You. I am giving You full control. Fill me until I am overflowing. In Jesus's name. Amen.

DAY 6

The Enemy of Faith

Now the serpent was more cunning than any beast of the field which the Lord God had made. And he said to the woman, "Has God indeed said, 'You shall not eat of every tree of the garden'?"

Genesis 3:1

IS DOUBT SINFUL? ASK THE AMERICAN SOLDIERS STATIONED IN Japan during World War II. They tuned their radios into Tokyo Rose and her popular propaganda. Many female radio personalities taunted the soldiers about unfaithful wives back home and a nation that had turned its back on them. Imagine a world without today's internet keeping us connected, and you will have some idea about the low morale these doubts created.

Satan hasn't changed his playbook since the garden of Eden. He still attacks us with his fiery darts of doubt. Unlike Eve, we must seek cover behind our shields of faith (Ephesians 6:16).

If Eve, a perfect woman with a perfect marriage to the perfect husband living in paradise fell for the element of doubt, we haven't got a chance. Thanks to Jesus Christ, we have the victory.

Our enemy, the father of lies, manipulates God's Word. Compare the above verse with God's command: "But of the tree of the knowledge of good and evil you shall not eat" (Genesis 2:17). Satan put a negative spin on God's command. He still does this today to make us believe God holds out on us. If the enemy can get us to doubt God just a little, he has succeeded in his plan.

God's best is better than the best the world offers.

Satan's deception worked in the garden, and it has worked down through the centuries. Why should he bother to change his plot?

Do you see the significance of knowing Scripture? Friend, I hope you can quote Bible verses better than I, but if not, we have the written Word. We must open our Bibles and place our thoughts under the lens of God's truth. If Eve had only paused to compare deception with God's actual words, life would have turned out quite different. But Eve had already believed the lie, thinking God had refused to give her every blessing possible.

Doubt may not be sinful, but it is dangerous.

Don't allow Satan to win at his age-old game any longer. We can learn from Eve's mistakes and live in obedience to God.

Ponder and Practice

Compare Isaiah 14:14 with Genesis 3:5. The verse in Isaiah gives us a glimpse into the mind of Lucifer when God cast him out of heaven along with one-third of the angels who rebelled with him against God. Do you see how Satan placed his own thought in Eve's mind? That's sobering, knowing the enemy's thoughts have lodged in my mind, and some may still linger. These thoughts may be the ones that lead to doubt, fear, or worry.

List some thoughts that Satan might have planted in your own mind. Hint: they are lies.

_____

_____

_____

Now list the truths for each of the above lies.

_____

_____

_____

In Genesis 3:7, we find the three doors to temptation and sin. Compare that verse to 1 John 2:16. What parallels do you observe? How can you apply this to your life?

_____

_____

_____

Create a plan to defeat the temptations and sin you might be battling.

_____

_____

_____

Prayer

Lord God, cleanse my mind with the blood of Jesus from all the thoughts planted by the enemy. Help me not doubt You when the enemy hisses in my ear. Surround my mind with the helmet of salvation. Thank You, in the name of Jesus. Amen.

DAY 7

The Three Rs to a Spirit-Filled Mind

For the weapons of our warfare are not carnal but mighty in God for pulling down strongholds, casting down arguments and every high thing that exalts itself against the knowledge of God, bringing every thought into captivity to the obedience of Christ.

2 Corinthians 10:4–5

"CAROLYN, YOU'RE AN IDIOT!" I BERATED MYSELF FOR LEAVING MY backpack filled with groceries on the city bus. I felt more like an idiot when I asked Timmy to leave work and chase down the bus to retrieve my backpack.

While making the trip to Walmart, I had read something about negative self-talk. I had just committed to avoid it only hours earlier.

My mind raced, seeking for a truth from the Bible to replace the negativity. I turned to Ephesians chapter 1. This passage gave me many names to call myself besides idiot. Words like *blessed* and *forgiven*. As I spoke God's truth over myself, I believed it.

Do you talk trash to yourself? Whether it comes from our enemy, our lips, or those of some thoughtless person, we will stop listening to the lies today. Let's unpack these verses and discover how to think with a Spirit-filled mind. Only God can have victory over strongholds. A stronghold is the sum of deceptive thoughts and perceptions—stinking thinking.

Our enemy has erected a high thing—a dividing wall—in our minds. He owns some real estate there, and this wall prevents godly thoughts from spilling over to his side.

What is our part in this battle for our minds? We implement the three Rs:

- Reveal the lie.
- Remove it.
- Replace the lie with God's truth.

I had grown so accustomed to my stinking thinking that I didn't recognize it as a lie. When I revealed it, I realized I'm not an idiot. I just made a mistake. It takes time to turn this into a habit.

Next, remove that thought. Send it an eviction notice and refuse to allow it to lodge in the fertile soil of your mind.

Finally, replace it with God's truth. Find Scriptures that contradict that particular lie. Speak truth over yourself. Words are powerful, and we need words of truth.

Lies are temporal, but God's truth is eternal.

We've covered a lot of ground today, but friend, this process brings emotional healing. It changes our perspective on everything. I know you can do this, because with God's help, nothing is impossible.

Ponder and Practice

Turn back to the list of negative thoughts you created on day four. Take one thought at a time and implement the three Rs. Don't rush through the process. Allow yourself time to do this foundational work, even if it takes several days. The goal of this book is to break free from negativity. When a contractor builds a house, his most important work is the foundation. A house is only as good as the foundation it sits on. The same applies spiritually.

We want a firm foundation, so do this exercise in prayer, and don't rush it.

Reveal the lie you will address first. Like me, you may not currently believe that negative thought is a lie. Admit to yourself that it is.

Write down the lie.

_____

_____

_____

Remove the lie from your thoughts. Replace it with a truth from Scripture. Write down the truth here.

_____

_____

_____

You can use a journal if you need more room so you can correct every deceitful thought.

Prayer

God, You are mighty, and I need You to pull down these strongholds and high things in my mind. Reveal the lies to me and lead me to Your truth. In Jesus's name. Amen.

DAY 8

Changed from Within

*And do not be conformed to this world, but be transformed
by the renewing of your mind, that you may prove what
is that good and acceptable and perfect will of God.*

Romans 12:2

CHRISTIANS HAVE SOMETHING IN COMMON WITH POPCORN. HEAT
turns the moisture within each kernel to steam. As the steam expands
against the external shell, it pops. That hard kernel of corn has transformed into a soft, edible piece of popcorn.

Dr. Tony Evans explains that the fire of the Holy Spirit transforms
believers in a similar fashion. The changes taking place internally
show up externally in our behavior and personality.[4]

God saved me at age thirty-three, and the world had already
polluted my mind. I needed a thorough cleaning of my thought
processes. I couldn't stop at sweeping out the sinful thoughts. I also
had to remove the fear-provoking thoughts along with all those that
created worry, discouragement, and every form of emotional bondage.
That took some time. As a baby Christian, I didn't know the enemy
had cluttered my head with negativity that caused toxic thoughts
and emotions.

A God-surrendered will leads to a God-surrendered mind.

Friend, it doesn't happen overnight. First, we must stop conforming to the world. Through the Holy Spirit, God renews our minds, but

43

we must be willing participants. As long as we continue conforming to the world, we block our minds from the transformational work of the Spirit.

The Greek word for transformation is the word *metamorphous*. In English, metamorphosis is the process by which a caterpillar changes into a butterfly and the process by which a kernel of corn becomes popcorn. The change takes place on the inside, but it soon becomes evident on the outside.

As I surrendered my will to God, the Holy Spirit cleansed my mind. His desires became my desires.

We can continue in our self-willed ways, but when we submit to God's will, transformation takes place. Walking by faith requires walking in the Spirit. God begins renewing our minds so we can have the mind of Christ.

Ponder and Practice

Read 2 Corinthians 3:18. What insight does this verse give you about transformation?

_____

_____

_____

How important is spending time with God for the transformational and renewing process? How can you carve out that time in your life?

_____

_____

_____

According to Romans 12:2, what are the benefits of transformation? What benefits do you still desire for yourself?

_____

_____

_____

"Therefore gird up the loins of your mind, be sober, and rest your hope fully upon the grace that is to be brought to you at the revelation of Jesus Christ" (1 Peter 1:13).

The command to be sober implies being stable. When I am trapped in emotional bondage, I am anything but stable. Peter sums it up with our hope. Where does our hope rest? What do you need to relinquish to the will of God?

_____

_____

_____

Prayer

Heavenly Father, these deceitful thoughts and emotions hold me in bondage. Free me from these chains that bind me. Renew my mind so I can have the mind of Christ. In Jesus's name. Amen.

DAY 9

Putting on the Armor

Put on the whole armor of God, that you may be able to stand against the wiles of the devil.

Ephesians 6:11

BEFORE I LEAVE THE HOUSE, I GET DRESSED, AND I GRAB IVA'S harness and leash. At Guiding Eyes, the school where I got Iva, the first things we learned included attaching the harness and leash. The right equipment is essential for a guide dog team. Plus, it says, *I'm working.*

As believers under fire, we must learn to dress in our essential armor. It sends a message to Satan. *Don't mess with me!*

The belt of truth literally sets us free. A Roman soldier couldn't fight with his tunic flapping around his legs while he held his sword and shield. He tucked that tunic up under his belt. The large, heavy belt held his sword and was firmly attached to his breastplate.

Our spiritual belts of truth stabilize us. Fickle emotions and deception enslave us, but the truth sets us free. Truth stabilizes us because it never changes.

Righteousness equals right living. The breastplate covered the vital organs like the heart, which represents the seat of our emotions and will. Wrong living attracts demonic activity. Clearly, we want to avoid sin. It hinders our prayers and blessings.

What is the opposite of emotional turmoil? Peace. Roman soldiers wore thick leather sandals with hobnails in the bottom to grip the ground, an ancient form of cleats. We need to stand our ground when we engage in hand-to-hand spiritual combat, just like the ancient Romans.

Take up the shield of faith. When we obediently live out God's promises, we walk by faith. Some people call the shield of faith the "fear extinguisher"—such a fitting name since it quenches the fiery arrows of fear, worry, doubt, and everything we plan to conquer in this study.

Satan can't have our souls, so he attacks our minds daily. The helmet of salvation protects our minds from his lies and negativity.

Our only offensive weapon is the sword of the Spirit. God's authoritative Word has power to transform, and it delivers swift blows to Satan—two things we will accomplish throughout this study.

God gave us a sword because He knew we'd have battles.

God knew the warfare we would face. Don't begin your day without prayer that includes all six pieces of God's armor. We dress through prayer. Each morning, as you physically dress, get spiritually dressed through prayer.

Ponder and Practice
Turn back to yesterday's journal section. What similarities do you see between the belt of truth and 1 Peter 1:13?

_____

_____

_____

"And you shall know the truth, and the truth shall make you free" (John 8:32). What can the truth set you free from today?

_____

_____

_____

Read Proverbs 4:23 and Jeremiah 17:9. What observations can you make about the heart (your emotions)?

_____

_____

_____

"You will keep him in perfect peace, whose mind is stayed on You, because he trusts in You" (Isaiah 26:3). What is the key to peace according to this verse?

_____

_____

_____

Look back at Day 3. What is the definition of faith? What can you do differently today to walk by faith?

_____

_____

_____

Read Hebrews 4:12. What does the Word of God do, according to this verse? How can you apply this truth to your own faith walk?

_____

_____

_____

Prayer

Lord Jesus, remind me of Your truth today as I encounter lies. Help me live righteously and holy today. Forgive me for my sin. Fill me with peace when panic arises. Increase my faith so I can walk in it. Guard my mind with Your helmet, and help me wield the sword swiftly. In Jesus's name. Amen.

DAY 10

Spiritual Anorexia

For "who has known the mind of the Lord that he may instruct Him?" But we have the mind of Christ.

1 Corinthians 2:16

ANOREXIA HAS THE HIGHEST MORTALITY RATE OF ALL MENTAL illnesses.[5] The disease robs a person of vital nourishment. Sadly, many Christians suffer from spiritual anorexia, eating one meal on Sunday and nothing throughout the week.

As spiritual infants, we crave the pure milk of the Word (1 Peter 2:2). Spiritual maturity occurs when we graduate from a milk diet to a meat diet.

A milk diet includes biblical doctrine. It gives us knowledge. A milk Christian can quote verses and even exceed a meat Christian in knowledge. Head knowledge alone doesn't transform lives. It's just information.

Meat-eating Christians go beyond head knowledge to discernment. The Holy Spirit teaches us by shedding light on the Bible as we read. The word used for *mind* can be translated as *understanding*. Meat eaters gain the understanding that milk Christians lack.

Perhaps you ask, *How can I know if I'm a meat eater?* Are you teachable? When light exposes error, do you act on it? The Holy Spirit won't illuminate the mind set on her own will.

In his book, *Life Essentials*, Tony Evans says that discernment accounts for the difference between biblical knowledge and spiritual understanding.[6] Have you ever known someone who has the ability to unlock the deeper meaning of a verse or passage? That's discernment, but it's not reserved for preachers. The Holy Spirit gives discernment to anyone who seeks an intimate relationship with Christ.

To overcome the emotions that bind us, we must eat a healthy spiritual diet of meat. Pattern your life after Mary, who sat at the feet of Jesus. We can also fashion our lives after the apostle John. He loved Christ so much that he leaned on His chest at the Last Supper, diligent to rightly divide the truth (2 Timothy 2:15).

Where are you on the road to spiritual maturity? Has today's message whet your appetite for the ability to discern the Word of God? Can you commit to prayer and meditation?

Many think they can switch their faith on anytime they need it, but as you have learned today, it takes time and diligence. Are you ready to create a plan that activates your faith?

Ponder and Practice

Read Hebrews 5:11–14. The author of Hebrews stops his teaching in verse 11, because his readers have become "dull of hearing," as the New King James Version (NKJV) puts it. The New Living Translation (NLT) reads "spiritually dull and don't seem to listen." The New International Version (NIV) says "because you no longer try to understand." Look at some more translations and jot down their wording.

_____

_____

_____

Instead of progressing in spiritual growth, the Hebrews had regressed. Where are you on this journey?

_____

_____

_____

Warren Wiersbe describes milk as Christ's finished work on the cross and meat as the work Christ is doing in heaven now.[7] What observations can you gather from that comparison?

_____

_____

_____

Moving forward, we will build on what we have learned in this first section. Make sure you have implemented all changes now before moving ahead.

Prayer

Lord Jesus, help me know You like Mary and John did. Guard the new schedule I have created for Bible reading and prayer. Teach me Your Word through the Holy Spirit. Open my eyes to Your truth. In Jesus's name. Amen.

PART II

Feeling Unloved, Inadequate, Jealous, and Insecure

DAY 11

God Can't Love Me

*Greater love has no one than this, than
to lay down one's life for his friends.*

John 15:13

SO YOU DOUBT GOD'S LOVE? MAYBE JUST A LITTLE OR MAYBE A LOT.
Perhaps you feel like you have committed the unforgivable sin. If
God loved the apostle Paul, who murdered Christians before God
saved him (Acts 8:1–3), why wouldn't God love you? If Jesus expressed
love by washing the feet of Judas hours before he betrayed Him, why
wouldn't God love you?

Can we grasp the depths of God's love? I never doubted His love,
but often I've grown complacent about it. Since childhood, I knew God
loved me, but my appreciation for something so familiar often fades.

Paul never questioned God's love. His epistles display his grat-
itude for God's love.

Judas never understood God's love, or he would have never
betrayed Jesus. That's why it's so important that we comprehend the
love of God. Not that we will betray Him like Judas, but so we don't
betray ourselves.

We can walk by faith because our faith isn't in ourselves but in God.
We need a clear picture of God's love since we place our trust in Him.

First, Christ died for us. Look at today's verse. No love can be
greater than to lay down one's life for one's friends. The One you place

your trust in died for you. Since He gave His life for you, wouldn't He take care of you? Meditate on that.

In the next verse, Jesus said that He no longer calls us servants, but friends. The Greek word for *friend* meant a friend at court. Warren Wiersbe explains that it included the inner circle around a king.[8] Friend, we have been placed in the inner circle of King Jesus.

You'll never make God stop loving you.

Never doubt the love of God again. He loves you because He created you. He died for you because He loves you. People will leave you, but not Jesus. Husbands, fathers, and even our children can abandon us, but the love of God is from everlasting to everlasting (Jeremiah 31:3).

We will either be graspers of God's love or grabbers for people's love. If we grasp the full love of Christ, we won't grab at other things to fill us.[9]

Ponder and Practice

Read Paul's prayer in Ephesians 3:17–19. Look at the phrase "rooted and grounded in love." *Rooted* is an agricultural term. Plants and trees with roots that grow deep and wide can weather storms better due to their stability. God's love should stabilize us, especially during storms. *Grounded* is an architectural term referring to the foundation of a building. Let's look at how we can apply these terms to God's love.

How does the knowledge of God's love stabilize you?

_____

_____

_____

Notice that Paul also prays for the Ephesians to comprehend the immeasurable love of God. That is my prayer for you today.

Let's apply the three Rs to God's love:

Reveal the lie: God doesn't love me because . . .

_____

_____

Remove the lie by crossing it out.
Replace it with a truth from the Bible:

_____

_____

_____

Prayer

Lord, help me grasp Your love instead of grabbing at worldly things or people who can never fulfill me like You can. I love You, Lord. Thank You for Your unique love and Your sacrificial death. Amen.

DAY 12

Who Defines You?

But God, who is rich in mercy, because of His great love with which He loved us . . . made us alive . . . and raised us up together, and made us sit together in the heavenly places in Christ Jesus.

Ephesians 2:4–6

WOULD YOU HAVE BELIEVED IT IF SOMEONE HAD TOLD YOU SEVERAL years ago that you could be in two places at the same time? I can hop online and join a Zoom call anywhere in the world. While I physically sit here in Virginia, I can show up in Washington, Colorado, and even England.

Would this surprise the apostle Paul who penned the letter to the Ephesians? I doubt it, since he believed in being in two places at the same time. Let's start at the beginning of verse 4.

God loved us with a great love. God loves us today, but Paul wants us to understand that long ago, God did some things because He loved us.

God poured out His mercy on us, and not just some mercy. He is rich in mercy. He loved us to the degree that He had pity on us.

Alongside His mercy, He gave us grace—undeserved favor. Mercy means we don't get what we deserve, but grace gives us what we never deserved. All of this because He loved us.

Verse 5 explains that we were dead in sin. God made us alive in Christ. Dead people can't do anything to help themselves, but God raised us with Christ. Then He did something that will blow our minds when we understand it. He even used the word *together* twice in verse 6 so we could never question that we sit together with Christ in heavenly places.

As I pound out these words on my computer, I sit in my living room, but spiritually, I sit with Christ in the heavenly places. All because of God's great love.

When God saved us, He began sanctifying us. Why is that important?

God refines us, so He gets to define us.

We don't have to wait until we reach heaven to receive heavenly blessings. We can have it all now once we realize where we are positioned spiritually.

God didn't stop at raising us from death to life. He went one step further. He exalted us to sit with Jesus Christ in the heavenly places. With your feet firmly planted on earth, start living like you're seated with Christ.

Ponder and Practice

How do you define yourself? How does the world define you?

_____

_____

_____

Take some time to pray and reflect on your spiritual position in heavenly places. Read Ephesians chapter 1:3–14. Write down some of the words God uses to define you in these verses.

_____

_____

_____

Start identifying yourself as God identifies you.

Read Ephesians 1:21–23. Since we are seated with Christ in the heavenly places, who is under us (Ephesians 1:21)?

What are we lacking according to these verses?

_____

_____

_____

Consider the armor of God: the belt of truth, the breastplate of righteousness, the shoes of peace, the shield of faith, the helmet of salvation, and the sword of the Spirit. How can you use any or all of these when the enemy lies about who you are and your position next to Jesus in heavenly places?

_____

_____

_____

Prayer

Heavenly Father, thank You for Your great love, Your rich gifts of mercy, grace, and salvation. I don't quite grasp this spiritual positioning, but I ask You to make it real to me. In Jesus's name. Amen.

DAY 13

God Loves the Unlovable

Then she conceived again and bore a son, and said, "Because
the Lord has heard that I am unloved, He has therefore
given me this son also." And she called his name Simeon.

Genesis 29:33

HOW DO YOU KNOW SOMEONE LOVES YOU? DO THEY BRING YOU
chocolates or flowers? Do they spend time with you? Do you measure
love by what someone does for you? If so, look at what God has done.

As a visually impaired girl, I craved love with an insatiable appetite. Nobody wanted to hang out with the girl who couldn't see. After
God saved me, years passed before I appreciated God's love more than
the love of people. With the exception of my husband, I struggled
with feelings of rejection.

Jacob loved Rachel, but Rachel's father tricked Jacob. Instead of
marrying the love of his life, Jacob realized the next morning that he
had married Rachel's older sister, Leah. Long story short, Jacob ended
up with two sisters as his wives.

Leah must have lacked Rachel's beauty. The Bible says she had
weak eyes without any further explanation.

God knew Jacob never loved Leah, and He opened her womb, but
He closed Rachel's womb. God cares about the affairs of our hearts. He
showed Leah compassion when Jacob didn't. Does that comfort you?

God also blesses the unloved. He blessed Leah with a son. Leah
believed beyond a doubt that Jacob would love her after she gave him

his firstborn son, but he didn't. Jacob didn't love Leah after her second son, her third son, or even her fourth son.

Leah strived to win her husband's affections, but she never appreciated the love of her heavenly Father. She grew weary in a loveless relationship, and she hoped Jacob would at least become attached to her. She named her third son Levi. In Hebrew, Levi sounds like the word *attached*.

Out of desperation, Leah hoped for acceptance since she couldn't earn Jacob's love. Finally, Leah praised God by naming her fourth son Judah, meaning *the praise of the Lord*.

Stop beating on the door of man's love and walk through the door of God's love.

Can you see yourself in Leah? I have experienced the same striving and desperation. How many times do we settle for less than in relationships, allowing these relationships to define us? All the while, God showers us with His love, and we miss out on the greatest love of all.

Ponder and Practice

How do you think Leah felt in a loveless marriage?

_____

_____

_____

In what relationships have you felt unloved?

_____

_____

_____

"When the LORD saw that Leah was unloved, He opened her womb; but Rachel was barren" (Genesis 29:31).

When have you experienced God's blessing when you thought He didn't care?

_____

_____

_____

Why might we continue striving in toxic relationships?

_____

_____

_____

Read Deuteronomy 21:15–17. What does this passage reveal about God's love and concern for the unloved?

_____

_____

_____

Spend time in prayer, asking God to direct you concerning all your responses to the questions above. We need to understand God loves us and He cares about our relationships. What changes is He directing you to make about your attitudes and your relationships?

_____

_____

_____

Prayer

Father, You love me like no other, no matter what I've done in the past, or what I do today. Forgive me for not appreciating Your love as I strive for human affection. Surround me with people who love me and redirect those who may be toxic. In Jesus's name. Amen.

DAY 14

The Competition of Comparison

Then Rachel said, "With great wrestlings I have wrestled with my sister, and indeed I have prevailed." So she called his name Naphtali.

Genesis 30:8

I DIDN'T REALIZE I HAD A COMPARISON PROBLEM UNTIL I BEGAN reading about it. The Holy Spirit stomped my toes. Not only does comparison lower our self-esteem, but it can also create envy.

Dawn didn't seek speaking engagements. They flowed effortlessly to her. I had business cards, a website, recommendations, and a speaking coach but few invitations. Outwardly, I supported Dawn, but inwardly, she became my competition. I picked her messages apart, finding fault with them.

The two sisters, Leah and Rachel, competed for Jacob's love. Each one fumed with anger when she couldn't give Jacob a child. When Leah had given birth to four sons, Rachel gave her maid to Jacob to bear children for her. When Naphtali was born, Rachel declared victory. Their competition never ended until Rachel died giving birth to her second son, Benjamin.

These two sisters chose the worldly way to handle their problems, not God's way. They wrestled, meaning *twisted* in the Hebrew. When Rachel prevailed, she felt she had power over Leah. She named the maid's son Naphtali, "my wrestling."

We walk in victory when we choose compassion over comparison.

What if these ladies hadn't conformed to the world? What if they had chosen compassion instead of comparison? They might have enjoyed a large loving family together. "Comparison is the thief of joy," observed Theodore Roosevelt.[10]

Both sisters chose lifestyles of competition instead of resting in the joy of the Lord. I wrestled internally instead of sharing in Dawn's blessings.

When we compare ourselves with another woman, we appear to ourselves either better than or less than. Either way, we have invited the devil in. We have created a wrong view of self. If we view ourselves as less than, we nurture insecurities.

Is anyone enticing the green-eyed monster to rear his ugly head? As you scroll through social media, do you make critical remarks about yourself? Let's take our comparison to the cross and leave it. Ask God to renew our minds. Comparison ends with confession and repentance.

Ponder and Practice
Read James 3:13–18. Look closely at verse 14 in your favorite translation. Most versions translate it using the phrases "bitter jealousy" and "selfish ambition." The Passion Translation substitutes "competition" for selfish ambition.

God wants us to use heavenly wisdom, as described in verses 17–18.

Ask God to reveal any spirit of comparison or competition in your life so you can repent. What observations can you make that apply to your life from this passage?

_____

_____

_____

What can you do in your situation to incorporate the wisdom described in verses 17–18?

_____

_____

_____

Seeing the ugliness of comparison in our lives doesn't make an uplifting Bible study. Once God delivers us from this stronghold, we will live a life of joy, being comfortable and satisfied in our own skin. I am cheering you on.

Prayer

Lord God, forgive me for the spirit of comparison and competition. Help me see myself as the masterpiece You created and help me live in peace and compassion with others instead of striving to be someone I am not. In Jesus's name. Amen.

Trouble in the Twelve

*But not so among you; on the contrary, he who is greatest among you,
let him be as the younger, and he who governs as he who serves. For
who is greater, he who sits at the table, or he who serves? Is it not he
who sits at the table? Yet I am among you as the One who serves.*

Luke 22:26–27

I WHISPERED TO MY FRIEND SITTING NEXT TO ME, "THAT'S A HORRI-
ble beginning."

She hushed me. We were attending a women's conference
together, and I gave my harsh critique. Several months later, she came
to my house to visit, and I confessed.

"Do you remember what I told you at the ladies meeting?"

"I don't remember."

I angled myself to face her. "God showed me that my true motive
for criticism revolved around looking greater in your eyes."

My comparison revealed the horrific sins of pride and world-
liness. This reminds me of our Scriptures for today. Disputes arose
within the twelve disciples concerning who would be greater in the
kingdom. Who would sit at the right hand of Christ? Even on the
night of Jesus's arrest, they bickered like gentiles, and Jesus called
them out on it.

Jesus explained that the greater would be treated as the younger.
Then Jesus pointed out that He had served them when He washed

their feet. In verse 30, Jesus promised they'd all sit at His table in His kingdom.

Jesus modeled the life of a servant, and since we desire a life that honors Christ, we must follow in His steps. In his commentary on Luke, Warren Weirsbe states that servants don't argue about who is greater, because a godly servant will always see himself as the least. If we follow Jesus's example, the cross will always come before the crown.[11]

Today, I congratulated several authors on their accomplishments, and it felt good. I'm thankful God has dealt with me on my sinful attitudes, because sin hinders our blessings. Now I prefer playing the role of cheerleader instead of the competitor.

Is the comparison trap stealing your joy? Ask God to set you free and adopt the wisdom of John the Baptist, willing to decrease and wanting Christ to increase.

Ponder and Practice

Read John 3:25–30. What observations can you make about comparison from this passage?

_____

_____

_____

God wants His daughters to demonstrate humility, but not to the degree that we think negatively of ourselves. Comparison affects each of us differently. If you have fallen into the comparison trap, write out the three Rs to deal with it.

Reveal the lie:

_____

_____

_____

Remove the lie, and replace it with God's truth:

_____

_____

_____

Using each piece of the armor of God, find a Bible verse to combat comparison. Refer to this when you sense the pangs of comparison.

Belt of truth:

_____

_____

Breastplate of righteousness:

_____

_____

Shoes of peace:

_____

_____

Helmet of salvation:

_____

_____

Shield of faith:

_____

_____

Sword of the Spirit:

_____

_____

Prayer

Lord Jesus, take this stronghold of comparison away from me. Tear it down, and help me cheer my sisters on, whether in ministry or in the secular world. In Jesus's name. Amen.

DAY 16

Stop Playing the Comparison Game

I will praise You, for I am fearfully and wonderfully made;
Marvelous are Your works, And that my soul knows very well.

Psalm 139:14

HAVE YOU EVER SCROLLED THROUGH FACEBOOK AND FOUND SEEDS of disillusionment beginning to take root? Photos of perfect family holidays and homes that look like they belong in a *Better Homes and Gardens* magazine create self-doubt. Do you ever compare yourself to a family member with the perfect husband and perfect kids along with a beautiful singing voice? Does your coworker have organization down to a science? Why can't my yard be perfectly manicured like my neighbor's?

As women, we tend to play the comparison game, and social media has added to our distress. How can we stop playing a game we never win?

We can have confidence in who we are because who we are is who God created us to be.

Let's turn to creation for some examples. God loves variety. Evergreens stay green all year, but a maple tree's leaves turn from green to vibrant reds and yellows before falling to the ground, leaving bare branches for the winter. Tulips, Easter lilies, and creeping phlox dazzle us with blooms of pink, white, and violet in the spring while yellow mums coordinate with orange pumpkins in the fall.

I am fearfully and wonderfully made, but we are all created in the image of God. We are all part of the body of Christ. Imagine if we switched your thumb with your big toe. Tying your shoes, opening a tight lid, and writing just became more difficult. We would walk off-balance and need a larger shoe.

Each part of the body is right where it needs to be and so is each part of the body of Christ. We all minister to others in different ways. Not everyone appreciates us, but we're not everyone's cup of tea, and that's okay.

Today, I encourage you to thank God for who you are. God designed you to be the unique individual you are. When we fall into the comparison game, we are not only doubting our self-worth, but we demonstrate a distrust in God. God made you to be you and no one else.

Each time you doubt yourself, use it as a reminder to thank God for who you are, because you are exactly who God created you to be.

Ponder and Practice

"For we are His workmanship, created in Christ Jesus for good works, which God prepared beforehand that we should walk in them" (Ephesians 2:10).

In some translations, the word *workmanship* is translated as *masterpiece* or *handiwork*. In the Greek, the word is *poiēma*. It means beautiful poem, and it looks like our English word *poem*. You are God's beautiful poem!

Friend, that is you: a masterpiece, fearfully and wonderfully created by God, and you are marvelous. How do you doubt yourself?

_____

_____

_____

How can you begin seeing yourself through God's eyes?

_____

_____

_____

Prayer

Lord, thank You for creating me as Your masterpiece, fearfully and wonderfully made. Help me stop seeing what everyone else has and appreciate myself for who You want me to be. Amen.

DAY 17

Four Steps to Feeling Secure

*No man shall be able to stand before you all the
days of your life; as I was with Moses, so I will be
with you. I will not leave you nor forsake you.*

Joshua 1:5

WHAT COULD A TERRORIST ATTACK, A LAYOVER, AND A GUIDE DOG
school have in common? The fear of flying into LaGuardia Airport in
New York City had dissipated, but the enemy never ceases.

Two weeks before I flew to New York to attend Guiding Eyes
for the Blind, I discovered I had a layover. All my insecurities about
flying resurfaced quickly. Then, within twenty-four hours of my flight,
another terrorist attack hit the Big Apple.

Joshua had just stepped into Moses's sandals—and what big
sandals they were. He had to lead the Israelites into the promised
land. In Joshua chapter 1, God gave Joshua some instructions. We
can follow the same four steps when we need to slam on the brakes
of insecurity.

First, God told Joshua to arise and go (Joshua 1:2). Insecurities
tend to keep our feet planted instead of moving forward. Focus on
what's ahead and not the past.

Next, God told them He has already given them the land, but
they would have to take possession of it. Imagine someone gives you
a check for one million dollars. Until you cash that check, you haven't

taken possession of the money. That check cannot change your life until you cash it.

We find the next step in our focal verse. People speak negativity over us, making us doubt our abilities. The enemies who inhabited the promised land intimidated the Israelites. God won't abandon us, so don't let anyone stand in your way.

Finally, we can rest secure in the Word of God. God told Joshua that His Word shall not depart from them. He commanded them to meditate on it day and night.

I trusted God with the flight. A friend of a friend met me for the layover. She escorted me directly to my next flight. She happened to be the chaplain at that airport. I had a safe arrival, and members from the school staff met me.

Security isn't you controlling your world. Security is your world being controlled by God. When we follow Joshua's steps, we can flourish in God's security. He's in control of it all.

Ponder and Practice

Read Joshua 1:1–9. Notice verse 3: "Every place that the sole of your foot will tread upon I have given you." Notice the verb tenses. *Will tread* is future tense, but *have given* connotes this happened in the past and its effect continues.

Has God given you something, perhaps a dream, you haven't taken possession of yet?

What stands in your way? What dreams have you not taken possession of?

How does the command and promise given to Joshua in verse six relate to your unpossessed gift?

_____

_____

_____

Friend, I know how difficult it is to overcome insecurities. Did Joshua chew on his lower lip, unsure of God's instructions? Maybe he did, but Joshua couldn't allow uncertainty to stop him, and neither can we. I encourage you to follow God's directions as Joshua did: Move forward. Take possession. Don't allow anyone to stop you. Stay in the Word.

What does God promise to those who stay tethered to the Bible in verse 8?

If you don't already have a consistent Bible study habit, create one now. Guard that time because the enemy will seek to distract you.

Prayer

Heavenly Father, help me as I move forward. Thank You for Your constant presence. It calms me as I take possession of what You have already declared as mine. In Jesus's name. Amen.

DAY 18

Who Am I?

Or who makes the mute, the deaf, the seeing, or
the blind? Have not I, the Lord?

Exodus 4:11

I COLLAPSED INTO A HEAP ON THE FLOOR AS A TORRENT OF TEARS covered my carpet. "God, why did You call me to write when I can't see to proofread?" When I self-published my first book, *Incense Rising,* I knew nothing about publishing. Imagine my shock when I realized I had to proof the manuscript in ten days. Within twenty-four hours, life had become unkind.

I needed my husband's help. I waited for him to return from his weekend trip to check on his brother, but he couldn't come home. Timmy found his brother on life support, and the doctors demanded Timmy stay in the area. I dared not tell him about the newest obstacle in my publishing path.

I needed his brother to revive. I needed my husband home. I needed God to miraculously correct the manuscript, but God had other plans.

When God called Moses to deliver Israel out of their oppression from Egypt, Moses doubted his abilities. He also doubted God.

With each excuse Moses offered, God had a response. *Who am I but a shepherd? They won't believe me. I'm not eloquent of speech.*

Have you ever uttered that question: *Who am I to handle this promotion? Who am I to serve in ministry? Who am I to raise my grandkids? Who am I to deal with this crisis?*

Has insecurity flourished as you list all your excuses? Moses appeared humble, but wounded pride can mimic a humble heart. Humility looks at God and not self—not even our list of limitations.

Moses delivered his people, dependent on God. He even gave some pretty good speeches.

God provided friends who proofed my manuscript, but my brother-in-law passed on to heaven.

My security rests in who God is and not who I am.

Friend, when insecurity threatens to overwhelm you, trust in God and not yourself. It's difficult to break an old habit. The devil wants us to doubt our abilities and doubt God also. He wants us to trust in money, people, and the world system to solve our problems. Trust in the One who created you and sustains you. I know with God you can do this.

Ponder and Practice

"So He said, 'I will certainly be with you. And this shall be a sign to you that I have sent you: When you have brought the people out of Egypt, you shall serve God on this mountain'" (Exodus 3:12).

What two promises did God give Moses in Exodus 3:12?

How can you apply either of those two promises to your life now?

_____

_____

_____

Which promises speak to your insecurities? If you can't think of any, look up Philippians 4:13 and Hebrews 13:5. They are my favorites!

_____

_____

_____

Let's apply the three Rs to Moses. What lies did he believe?

_____

_____

_____

Which lies do you believe concerning your insecurities?

_____

_____

_____

You know the next step by now. Remove the lie and replace it with a truth.

_____

_____

_____

How can you walk this out in your life beginning today?

_____

_____

_____

Prayer

Heavenly Father, my nerves get rattled when I look at the enormous task before me. Sometimes, my insecurities make me feel like a failure, but I know I am secure with You. I also know You equip me to accomplish whatever You place in my path. What I can't do myself, I can do with You. In Jesus's name. Amen.

DAY 19

When Someone Makes You Insecure

Let not your heart be troubled; you believe in God, believe also in Me.
John 14:1

HER WORDS CUT LIKE A KNIFE INTO MY HEART. SOMETHING I DID failed to meet her high standards of perfection. The door slammed behind her as I fumed, tired of never measuring up.

I had almost completed my study on insecurity and comparison for this book. But what do you do when someone else tosses out belittling comments like yesterday's garbage, leaving me feeling like that's where I belong?

"No one can make you feel inferior without your consent," according to Eleanor Roosevelt.[12] Replace the lie with the truth.

The truth was, God doesn't see me as a failure. He sees me as His beloved and accepted daughter. Christ has already conquered my insecurities on the cross, but what do you do when someone's jagged tongue slices into your wounded soul?

Friend, I imagine if we were sharing a cup of hot cocoa or coffee, you'd nod your head in agreement. We can't avoid these folks. We can't control them, but we can control our response. First, let's dry those tears, and go to the Word.

Jesus spoke today's verse as directions to His disciples just hours before His arrest. The heart acts as the hub for our emotions. First, Jesus told us not to allow troubled feelings to get us down.

Easier said than done, Jesus.

Sweet friend, we must remember Jesus experienced insult and injury. He knows exactly how we react, but He also knows how to overcome.

Believe in God. The Greek word for believe, *pisteuete*, means to entrust.

When flesh controls us, insecurity reigns. When the Spirit controls us, security remains.

We will believe God. We believe His Word. We believe what He says about us because He created us.

Ignoring pain seems impossible, but we can't allow people to rule our hearts when our hearts belong to God. What can man do? My security rests in God who loves me.

The enemy will shoot flaming arrows our way, but we hold the shield of faith. God gave us that shield because He loves us. He chose us, and He protects us with His sovereign hand. Trust God. He's all the security we need.

Ponder and Practice

Read Proverbs 3:5–8.

Who do you turn to first in times of precariousness? What does your response demonstrate about your confidence in God? Do you trust Him with *all* your heart?

_____

_____

_____

Verse 6 says we must acknowledge Him in all our ways. What is the result of completely trusting God and fully relying on Him?

_____

_____

_____

When God directs our paths, we can have confidence in the direction He takes us. The path may create some angst, but since it's His path, we shouldn't feel alarmed. What promise does verse 8 give us when we apply godly wisdom rather than earthly wisdom?

_____

_____

_____

Read Psalm 16. The belt of truth is our first piece of armor. What truths do you find in this psalm?

_____

_____

_____

Prayer

Lord, tongue lashings hurt, but You were not only insulted, You felt Your flesh rip open when they struck You with the cat of nine tails. You understand my pain. Help me to trust in Your truth and not the harsh voice of the world and the enemy. Help me recognize the devil, who is behind the toxic language of others. Remove these thoughts from the soil of my mind. In Jesus's name. Amen.

DAY 20

When I'm Inadequate

Then He commanded the multitudes to sit down on the grass. And He took the five loaves and the two fish, and looking up to heaven, He blessed and broke and gave the loaves to the disciples; and the disciples gave to the multitudes.

Matthew 14:19

DO YOU EVER FEEL YOU'RE NOT ENOUGH? EITHER YOU DON'T HAVE enough or, no matter what you do, it isn't sufficient. Feelings of uselessness threaten to overwhelm your tender heart. Confusion clouds your thoughts because you had prayed about this. Why can't I ever get it right?

The emotion of inadequacy can stem from a myriad of situations ranging from insufficient funds to the inability to accomplish a particular task.

God drew me to this passage during a season of disappointment. I felt broken, like the fish and bread, but where was the blessing? What about the miracle?

Before the five loaves and two fish experienced a miraculous multiplication process, Jesus blessed them. Then He broke them. Friend, the bread was broken in the hands of Jesus. No better place to be broken.

Months passed as I waited for the blessing. When it arrived, I didn't recognize it at first. God had to break me before He could use me. Like the bread and fish, I couldn't serve the multitudes until I was broken.

I discovered God had blessed me before breaking me. We don't recognize the blessing because we can't see the behind-the-scenes work of God.

God takes our not enough and makes it more than enough.

Now I can serve the multitudes. You might say, "Carolyn, I'm not serving multitudes." No, but the testimony of your broken-to-blessed experience will encourage others one person at a time.

I'm sure the little boy with his lunch that long-ago day felt inadequate when he offered it to Andrew. But can you imagine the story he told his mom when he went home that evening?

I don't know why you feel unqualified to tackle the incredible mountain standing before you, but God won't let you tackle it alone. Perhaps you feel useless or incomplete—just hang on! God is taking you to a place where you will be more than enough. Believe in Him because He equips you to do what He calls you to accomplish.

Ponder and Practice

Let's turn to the armor of God as we complete this study on insecurity. Look up the following verses: Matthew 6:31; John 14:1; Ephesians 6:10; Philippians 4:6; and Philippians 4:13. Select one or more for your belt of truth and sword of the Spirit. Write the verse on a sticky note so you can place it somewhere you'll see it often.

Read Romans 8:4–6. Meditate on these verses and pray through them as you apply the breastplate of righteousness and the shoes of peace.

_____

_____

_____

In what way did God speak to you from this passage?

_____

_____

_____

Which fiery darts is the enemy shooting at you? Name them and quench them with your shield of faith.

_____

_____

_____

Our remaining piece of armor is the helmet of salvation. The battle against insecurity is fought down on our knees and in our minds. Read 1 Corinthians 2:16. Spend some time in prayer as you read through today's verses.

Use today's verses as you pray, dressing in the armor. Which verses complete your battle plan?

_____

_____

_____

Prayer

Heavenly Father, I trust that my insecurities are doors You will open. You are working behind those doors right now, even though I can't see it. I believe You have given me the mind of Christ. I know when I'm not enough, You are more than enough. In Jesus's name. Amen.

PART III

Worry and Stress

DAY 21

Living like Birds

*Look at the birds of the air, for they neither sow nor
reap nor gather into barns; yet your heavenly Father
feeds them. Are you not of more value than they?*

Matthew 6:26

SEPTEMBER 18, 2006, QUALIFIES AS THE WORST DAY OF MY LIFE. MY
eighteen-year-old daughter moved out of the house and turned her
back on me. I bathed my pillow in tears as a blanket of depression
covered me. How could I know if she was safe when she refused to
talk to me? How could a worried momma cling to sanity in the midst
of heartache and abandonment?

Jesus might have motioned to a flock of sparrows as He stood on
the mountainside preaching. "Look at the birds." He used the birds
as an example for us to live by. They wake up singing. They don't fret
about finding the next worm. God feeds those birds every day.

Jesus asked the rhetorical question. "Are you not of more value
than they?" We know God values us much more. Christ shed His
precious blood for us. So why do we worry?

Satan's weapon of worry inflicts much damage. It keeps us awake
at night. It gives us headaches, raises our blood pressure, and may
lead to ulcers.[13] Worst of all, worry doubts God.

What kind of mother doesn't worry about her children even
when they grow up? The mom who trusts completely in God and

believes God takes care of her family. This momma has concerns, but concerns don't control her like worry does.

Eight years passed before I heard from my daughter. We're currently working on rebuilding our relationship. Learning to pray and not worry has freed me from the chains of Satan.

We worry when we are flesh driven. We trust God when we are spirit led.

Friend, what worries hold you captive today? Are you worried about a child, or is it a normal concern? Can you give that worry to God, who loves you? Can you trust in the Lord, "who is able to do exceedingly abundantly above all that we think or ask" (Ephesians 3:20)?

We can trust God because we know His character. God desires our confidence. When you're prone to worry, remember who you are and whose you are.

Ponder and Practice

Satan says we can't trust God because He holds out on us (Genesis 3:4–5). What does God's truth say in Psalm 34:17 and Psalm 94:19? These verses provide us Scripture for the belt of truth and the sword of the Spirit.

_____

_____

_____

Peace is a fruit of the Holy Spirit, but worry is fleshly. Read Jeremiah 17:5–9. Compare the man who trusts in the flesh with the man who trusts in the Lord.

_____

_____

_____

In what situations have you found your heart to be deceitful?

_____

_____

_____

We need the breastplate of righteousness because our hearts deceive us. When Satan attacks our hearts with worry, we doubt God.

"Therefore, if anyone is in Christ, he is a new creation; old things have passed away; behold, all things have become new" (2 Corinthians 5:17). We still live in a body of flesh which tends to worry, but we can wear the helmet of salvation to protect our minds. What is God impressing upon you today with this verse?

_____

_____

_____

Prayer

Lord, forgive me for doubting You when I worry. I confess this sin and ask You to help me stop living enslaved by Satan's weapon of worry. Help me escape the temptation of worry. In Jesus's name. Amen.

DAY 22

God Provides in Unusual Ways

But seek first the kingdom of God and His righteous-
ness, and all these things shall be added to you.
Matthew 6:33

AS IVA AND I ASCENDED THE STAIRS, SOMETHING FELT OFF. THE
steep stairs seemed more numerous than I remembered. Wasn't there
a landing between the steps before? It had been some time since we
had visited Gatlinburg.

A friendly couple greeted us as we reached the top of the steps.
They held the door for us. I paused before entering. "Excuse me, is
this Calhoun's?"

"No, but I can take you there."

"That's not necessary. It's one block back, right?" I began understanding where I missed the restaurant I wanted.

The kind gentleman left his wife standing at the door and began
escorting me down the steps. He insisted on walking me to Calhoun's.

"Do you know why I want to walk you to Calhoun's? I'm
the owner."

Imagine that! God provided someone to help me that day. As we
neared Calhoun's with the owner safely escorting me to our destina-
tion, I could hear the familiar sloshing of water.

I had missed Calhoun's because I had a temporary hearing loss
in one ear. Walking down the bustling sidewalk of Gatlinburg with

my weaker ear facing the restaurant, I never heard my audio cue. An audio cue provides valuable information to blind people, like signs do for sighted people. I never heard the familiar sound of water as the waterwheel rotated in front of the restaurant because my good ear faced the other way.

I wanted God to restore my hearing. I wanted God to enable me to help myself in these predicaments. But that's not putting God first like our verse commands.

Worry says I am in control, not God.

The hearing impairment created worry about my safety. I worried about missing those audio cues. Would I hear an oncoming car when I crossed the street? Just heal me, God, and I won't have to worry. God protected me according to His ways, not mine. Eventually, He healed me in His timing.

What troubles you today? Is it an out-of-control situation which God hasn't resolved? If you can relate to my desire for control, take a deep breath. Relinquish the reins to God. He loves and values you, and He always provides exactly what you need just when you need it.

Ponder and Practice
Understanding God's sovereignty helps us put the kingdom of God in first place.

"And we know that all things work together for good to those who love God, to those who are the called according to His purpose" (Romans 8:28). How has God used a bad experience for good?

_____

_____

_____

Is there something in your life you haven't given completely to God? Perhaps you want God to answer a prayer in a particular way. How can you release your control and trust God to answer in His way and in His time?

_____

_____

_____

Why do you think letting go is such a struggle? Could it be that we still believe the lie Satan told Eve in the garden that we can be like God?

_____

_____

_____

How can you let go today?

_____

_____

_____

Prayer

Lord, help me trust Your sovereign hand and stop trying to control my world. I want Your will and not mine. I also desire Your timing, and I need Your help with waiting, because I don't wait well. In Jesus's name. Amen.

DAY 23

Three Steps to a Worry-Free Life

*Be anxious for nothing, but in everything by prayer and suppli-
cation, with thanksgiving, let your requests be made known to
God; and the peace of God, which surpasses all understanding, will guard your hearts and minds through Christ Jesus.*

Philippians 4:6–7

I SLAMMED THE DRAWER SHUT AS IF THE BILL COULD ESCAPE AND
threaten me with worry. During Timmy's battle with leukemia, his
medical bills left me exhausted. We did the same song and dance each
time a bill arrived stating that insurance didn't cover this charge. Did
they forget they had covered the exact service last time? Each time, I
called them reminding them they had previously paid for that service.
They promised to review it, and as I filed the bill away, I gave it to God.

Eventually, they always paid the bill, but this repetitive
scene grew old.

This became my first victory over worry, and I turn to today's
passage whenever worry tempts me.

"Be anxious for nothing." I like the New Living Translation:
"Don't worry about anything; instead, pray about everything"
(Philippians 4:6 NLT).

Stop worrying and start praying. These two steps go hand-in-
hand. Our flesh loves holding onto worry. We will pray about it, but
we continue worrying as if we have any control over the situation. This

simple command directs us to refuse the temptation to fret. Instead, we will pray.

Our passage gives us a third step: give thanks. It's not enough to give the problem to God in prayer. We must believe He will handle our troubling situation. We trust Him to resolve it, and we thank Him for what He will do. We thank God for taking action. That's something worry cannot do.

Friend, when we put these three steps into practice—stop worrying, start praying, and give thanks—God promises us peace. Not an ordinary serenity, but an extraordinary calm—the peace of God. The world can't understand it. We've never known anything like it. The peace guards our hearts and minds. It protects our minds from anxious thoughts like the helmet of salvation. It even guards our hearts, the seat of our emotions. The peace of God and the breastplate of righteousness both shield our hearts.

Thankfulness is the channel through which tranquility flows.

Our problems don't disappear at *amen*, but peace floods our previously panicked hearts.

Ponder and Practice

You control concerns, but worry controls you. Let's practice these three steps to freedom from worry. The same steps can be applied to other emotions, such as stress and fear.

1. Stop worrying.
2. Start praying.
3. Thank God for resolving the problem.

What worries you today? Write out your prayer about your worries, giving them to God, and thank Him.

_____

_____

_____

Our three Rs are similar to the exercise you completed above, but it takes you into the Word of God. Write out the three Rs for the same worry.

1. Reveal the lie. What is the lie?

_____

_____

_____

2. Remove it.
3. Replace it with a truth from the Bible. Write that verse here, or you may choose the following verse, a truth from Jesus's sermon about worry in Matthew. "Therefore do not worry about tomorrow, for tomorrow will worry about its own things. Sufficient for the day is its own trouble" (Matthew 6:34).

_____

_____

_____

Prayer

Lord, forgive me for feeling anxious. I am giving these worries to You right now. Thank You for all You will do. Thank You for helping me remember You are sovereign. Your peace awaits me. In Jesus's name. Amen.

DAY 24

Are We Balancing Busyness?

But Martha was distracted with much serving, and she approached Him and said, "Lord, do You not care that my sister has left me to serve alone? Therefore tell her to help me."

Luke 10:40

ATTENDING MULTIPLE VIRTUAL WRITERS CONFERENCES SEEMED like a good idea in the year of lockdowns. But I left each conference carrying a new weight on my shoulders. Run Facebook ads, start a YouTube channel, and build your email list. My to-do list grew with each meeting. I began experiencing burnout, thinking I needed to accomplish everything now.

Meet Martha. She reminds me of my mom. She loved inviting people to dinner without considering all the work. Like Momma, Martha spent all her time in the kitchen while everyone else congregated in the living room.

Was Martha resentful because her sister, Mary, sat at Jesus's feet? Was she overwhelmed with cooking for Jesus and twelve disciples? Had she gone just a bit overboard with an elaborate dish?

When stress arises, we turn to Jesus, but Martha's flawed thinking appeared when she asked Jesus to rebuke Mary.

"And Jesus answered and said to her, 'Martha, Martha, you are worried and troubled about many things. But one thing is needed, and Mary has chosen that good part, which will not be taken away from her'" (Luke 10:41–42).

I identify with Martha, worrying with elaborate and unnecessary details. The enemy loves us Marthas! We fall for his tactic of distraction. In the Greek, the word means *to be over-occupied about something*. I prefer the quietness of sitting at the feet of Jesus rather than the anxiety of busyness because a servant's heart gets preoccupied.

We can't sit with Jesus while we serve Jesus. We must strategize to balance Martha's load with a Mary heart.

One of my favorite childhood toys, a spinning top, sat upright twirling around until it fell over on one side. Our lives resemble that spinning top when we fail to balance them. They will spin like teetering tops until we collapse.

I took some time off, and I gave my load to Jesus. I start my day in His Word as His daughter before I pull out my laptop and serve Him.

Friend, do you stress over details like Martha, or do you resemble Mary? Amid the laundry, cleaning, meals, paying bills, and serving the Lord, make time to sit with Jesus. Warren Weirsbe explains this concept nicely: "What we do with Christ is far more important than what we do for Christ."[14]

Ponder and Practice

"So we don't look at the troubles we can see now; rather, we fix our gaze on things that cannot be seen. For the things we see now will soon be gone, but the things we cannot see will last forever" (2 Corinthians 4:18 NLT).

What light does this verse shed on Jesus's remark about Mary's choice?

_____

_____

When Satan cannot deceive us, he distracts us. I turned to this verse during my overwhelming seasons: "Casting all your care upon Him, for He cares for you" (1 Peter 5:7).

Rewrite this verse substituting your source of stress for the phrase *all your care.*

_____

_____

_____

"What we do with Christ is far more important than what we do for Christ." (Warren Weirsbe)[15]

If you set unrealistic goals or add elaborate details, what's one change you can make this week to reduce your load?

Let's apply the three Rs:

Reveal the lie:

Remove the lie and replace it with the truth:

Prayer

Lord, thank You for caring about all the mundane and not-so-mundane things that weigh me down. Today, I am naming each source of busyness and stress. Teach me how to balance busyness. Amen.

DAY 25

Don't Worship in the Kitchen

*But one thing is needed, and Mary has chosen that
good part, which will not be taken away from her.*

Luke 10:42

HOW OFTEN DO YOU WORSHIP AT THE KITCHEN TABLE? PERHAPS
every morning as you sip your coffee, reading your Bible. My table
reminds me of the high places where Israel worshipped their false
gods. I struggle with the idol of food when anxiety soars. Israel's high
places resembled a stage, so you see the similarity to a table.

I can picture Martha in the kitchen busy cooking. She peeks into
the living room and sighs. *Mary left all the work for me to finish alone.*
As stress intensifies, Martha begins sampling the meal. *The biscuits
turned out great! I have plenty.* She makes the excuse to sample a few
of them. Of course, she slathers on the butter.

God gave us an inexhaustible menu to enjoy, but He never
intended for food to become a substitute for Him. Satan tempted
Eve with food, and food has tempted us ever since the fall.

Here comes the part where I tell you I've found the answer to
our stress eating, but I haven't. Don't think of me as a hypocrite, just
a sister who hasn't conquered the distraction of doughnuts and fresh
bread. I know the truths, but like you, sweet friend, I have to commit
to walk them out.

Stress drives me to food, but I need to feast at the feet of Jesus.

Three things transpire when we sit at the feet of Jesus. First, we humble ourselves when we bow down at His feet. We put Christ first, above our desires. Yes, even before our desire for ice cream.

Next, feasting at the feet of Jesus puts us in His presence. Some blessings occur only at the feet of Jesus. We worship Him. We adore Him and not that chocolate candy.

Finally, when we feast at the feet of Jesus, we choose the good part, as Mary did. When we arise after sitting, we leave filled with peace and hope. When we finish off a bag of chips, we still have problems, plus some extra pounds, and no comfort.

Let's make the commitment to implement true worship instead of turning to the idol of food. Let's feast at the feet of Jesus.

Ponder and Practice

I've created a list of lies we tell ourselves about food. After each lie, find a truth to replace it. I did the first one as an example.

Lie: Food satisfies me.

Truth: "And Jesus said to them, 'I am the bread of life. He who comes to Me shall never hunger, and he who believes in Me shall never thirst'" (John 6:35).

Lie: I need to eat this while it's fresh.

Truth:

_____

_____

_____

Lie: Food is instant gratification.

Truth:

_____

_____

_____

Lie: Food is an escape.
Truth:

_____

_____

_____

What other lies do you believe about food? Replace each one with a truth.

_____

_____

_____

_____

_____

Prayer

Lord, remind me to read these truths and feast at Your feet before I seek solace in food. You are my only source for peace and hope. Amen.

DAY 26

Does Anyone Care About My Heavy Load?

And she approached Him and said, "Lord, do You not care that my sister has left me to serve alone? Therefore tell her to help me."

Luke 10:40

"I QUIT! I'M DONE WITH MINISTRY." THE MOMENT I DECLARED THOSE words, I knew I could never quit. Does the world of technology ever leave you feeling incompetent and irritable? Double that for a blind person navigating the World Wide Web. Add a hairline mistake on a book cover, and you have a recipe for the perfect storm.

The pressure had built up all day. Now I sat with a bag of chips and a box of tissues.

Martha felt like Jesus didn't care that Mary had abandoned her in the kitchen to prepare the meal alone. I felt like the Lord didn't care about my struggles with my website and the load that accompanies self-publishing on your own. Friend, today you might feel He doesn't care about your burdens, but let's stop believing that lie. Jesus does care, but do we care about the time we spend with Him? Perhaps I spent a few minutes praying this morning, but I spent hours on the computer accomplishing almost nothing.

My Jesus time must exceed my stress time.

Martha had the right idea. She went to Jesus with her heavy load. She spoke honestly as she asked Him to send Mary back into the kitchen. We can admire Martha's candor. I know I've waited too long to sit with Jesus when I criticize others like Martha did. I need to take a break and get alone with Him, especially in my busiest seasons.

When irritation creeps in, we tend to have a pity party. Our people don't applaud the scrumptious dinner on the table. No one offers to help wash the dishes. They don't appreciate their clean laundry. At work, the time we invested in a project goes unnoticed and unrewarded. We conclude they don't appreciate us.

Hit the brakes, and let's check the temperature of our quiet time, because when self-pity moves in, I need more time with Jesus.

Your stress may stem from a multitude of sources, but we still feel the same effects as Martha. We can exchange that fast-paced panic for peace when we choose the good part. Choose Jesus.

Ponder and Practice

We have concentrated on truth on previous days. Let's round out the rest of the armor of God, beginning with the breastplate of righteousness, which protects our hearts.

By the time we feel the effects of stress, we have doubted God and His goodness. We have believed the enemy's lie that God doesn't care. We might feel we don't deserve to turn to Christ, but that's what Satan wants.

Read Philippians 3:9. Where does our righteousness come from?

_____

_____

What does God see when He looks at us?

_____

_____

Read John 14:27. What command does Christ give here? What is the source of our peace?

_____

_____

_____

Now for the helmet of salvation. Read Philippians 4:8. What will you meditate on today?

_____

_____

_____

Raise up the shield of faith against every anxious thought and choose a Scripture for your sword to inflict injury to the enemy, who has brought anxiety, stress, and worry upon you.

_____

_____

_____

Prayer

Lord Jesus, I confess that I believed You didn't care. I know You care more than I realize. As I dress in Your armor, go before me. Thank You for the victory over this stress. Amen.

DAY 27

Correcting Flawed Behavior

Casting all your care upon Him, for He cares for you.
1 Peter 5:7

HAVE YOU EVER AWOKEN DREADING EVERYTHING YOU HAVE TO do? Once you loved doing this, but now it weighs you down. I love my work, but somehow my blessing had turned into a burden. I am a demanding person. My family will tell you this, but I demand more from myself than I do from others.

While taking a much-needed break, I concentrated on time management. I discovered that I cannot squeeze but so much into one twenty-four-hour day. The hours don't stretch like a snug pair of blue jeans.

I studied today's verse. The NIV says, "Cast all your anxiety on Him." The NLT says, "Give all your worries and cares to God." Jesus wants us to take all that worries us, all that stresses us, and our overloaded schedules and cast them on Him because He cares for us. The word *cast* connotes the idea of throwing something onto something else, like throwing a blanket onto a donkey.

Martha learned how to do this. When Lazarus died, Martha hurried to meet Jesus when she heard He had arrived in Bethany (John 11:20). In John chapter 12, we find Martha back in the kitchen serving while Mary anointed the feet of Jesus, but something had changed. Martha no longer stressed about the meal, and she didn't complain about Mary not helping her. Did Martha change her menu to something less time-consuming? Did she spend quality time with Christ earlier?

We don't have these answers. Perhaps Martha had learned to cast her cares on Jesus, knowing He cared for her. Previously, she felt like no one cared.

Before beginning my daily assignment, I must get in my daily alignment with Jesus.

Friend, could the answer to our overloaded schedules be spending time with Jesus? Time to cast our burdens on Him and time to soak in His calm before heading into the day's chaos.

Martha course corrected. When we see her with a houseful of people gathered for Lazarus's funeral, Martha left the guests and went to meet Jesus. I have also shut the door on demanding schedules and stress by prioritizing my Jesus time. Flawed behavior must be dealt with. How can you intentionally give Jesus the first portion of your day?

Ponder and Practice

Why do you pick up your burdens when you have cast them on Christ?

_____

_____

_____

Jesus wants to be our burden bearer. Read Matthew 11:28–30. What does Jesus promise to give you when you take your heavy load to Him?

What command does Jesus give in verse 29?

_____

_____

_____

What can you learn from Jesus? Take some time with this answer. Prayerfully consider His life. It could have been stressful, but we don't see Jesus struggling with anxiety until the garden of Gethsemane (Mark 14:34).

_____

_____

_____

Jesus, God in the flesh, needed time to pray in solitude. How does this speak to you?

_____

_____

_____

Prayer

Lord, each morning I want to wake up with joy and not dread for what the day holds. Help me see the joy and grasp it while I let something else wait for another day. Thank You for bearing my burdens and giving me rest. Amen.

DAY 28

Burnout

For he shall be like a tree planted by the waters,
Which spreads out its roots by the river,
And will not fear when heat comes;
But its leaf will be green,
And will not be anxious in the year of drought,
Nor will cease from yielding fruit.

Jeremiah 17:8

MY FEET COULDN'T CARRY ME TO THE ALTAR FAST ENOUGH. "Forgive me, Lord. I'm sorry!"

Tears fell like rain. The message about Martha and Mary had hit home. When had I worshipped like Mary? Writing books and speaking keeps a Martha girl busy—too busy to be like Mary.

You might not serve in ministry, but you know busyness. Early mornings and late nights leave you with little time or energy to sit with Jesus.

Unchecked, stress leads to burnout. In Jeremiah chapter 17, the prophet compares a desert bush to a tree planted by the waters. The desert shrub represents Judah, who trusted in themselves and their own strength, but the tree by the rivers depicts someone trusting in God.

The desert shrub inhabits isolated, parched places (Jeremiah 17:6). The tree planted by the river spreads out its roots as it grows. This productive tree bears fruit in the year of drought. Even the heat cannot dry up its green leaves.

Notice Jeremiah doesn't say the tree planted by the waters never endures heat and drought, but even in those seasons, this tree doesn't fear the heat nor will it be anxious.

Friend, we don't choose to ignore God, but life happens. Our parched souls thirst for the water of the Word.

By the time I reach burnout, I am trusting in myself to accomplish multiple tasks, and I have little time for God. My barren heart needed to soak in the water of the Word.

I gave God my schedule, and He gave me His wisdom when I sought it with a committed heart. Now I feel like the tree Jeremiah described in our focal verse.

When we drift from God, we don't notice the distance until we've drifted too far. If you feel the scorching heat of burnout, run back to the water. Drink in its refreshment.

Our productivity increases when we soak in the water of the Word rather than the isolated life of the wilderness. Jesus never intended for us to live in our own strength, but He wants us to rely on Him. Blessing comes to the one fully relying on God.

Ponder and Practice

"He shall be like a tree planted by the rivers of water, that brings forth its fruit in its season, whose leaf also shall not wither; and whatever he does shall prosper" (Psalm 1:3). God's definition of prosperity differs from that of the world. What indicates success in the world?

_____

_____

_____

A well-watered tree shows signs of nourishment. Do you consider yourself a healthy, well-nourished Christian? Why or why not?

_____

_____

_____

Healthy trees and Christians bear fruit. What fruit do your friends and family see you producing?

_____

_____

_____

Hydrated trees and Christians don't wither. What signs of spiritual decay, past or present, have you seen in your life? How can you prevent decay?

_____

_____

_____

Read the first two verses of Psalm 1. According to the psalmist, these practices lead to prosperity. What does prosperity look like to God?

_____

_____

_____

How are you prospering now?

_____

_____

_____

Prayer

Heavenly Father, I've been in the ashes of burnout. I don't want to return. Help me shield the time I set aside with You and soak in the water of the Word. I won't be anxious or fear the drought when I am nourished by You. In Jesus's name. Amen.

DAY 29

Conquering Stress

But at midnight Paul and Silas were praying and singing hymns to God, and the prisoners were listening to them. Suddenly there was a great earthquake, so that the foundations of the prison were shaken; and immediately all the doors were opened and everyone's chains were loosed.

Acts 16:25–26

DO YOU EVER FEEL LIKE YOU LIVE INSIDE A PRESSURE COOKER? YOU have appointments to keep, weekly shopping, and daily meals to prepare. We haven't begun to list all the demands from your job. Why is life so stressful?

The enemy applies pressure to Christians because he loves the effects of a pressure cooker lifestyle. Prayerlessness results from a full schedule. Those on-the-go prayers just don't comfort our racing hearts like we need. An overwhelmed life often leaves the Bible unopened from Sunday to Sunday. Joy escapes us, and hopelessness settles in.

Paul and Silas had set a woman free from demon possession, but her masters grew angry since they had profited from her fortune-telling skills. The Philippian magistrates imprisoned Paul and Silas after beating them. Unable to move with their legs stretched far apart and held in stocks, pain intensified by the minute. Heavy chains weighed their bruised and bloody bodies down.

The prisoners had no control over their situation, but they could control their reactions. Paul and Silas didn't stress out. They looked up.

Life's pressures are no match for God's presence.

In their darkest hour, at midnight, Paul and Silas began praying and singing hymns. God inhabited their praises and invaded their prison, setting them free.

Stress surrounds us like prison bars. Anxiety stretches us to the breaking point. The weight of too many requests drags us down like heavy chains. When the pressure of life increases, we must determine to meet it with prayer and praise.

Paul and Silas couldn't control their crisis, so they invited God in. We can't control life either. The toilet overflows, the car breaks down, or the boss bellows out impossible demands, and we can't hit a pause button to make it stop.

Friend, when tensions imprison you, turn to God like Paul and Silas did. He breaks the chains of anxiety and releases you from the confines of pressure. Ask God to invade your out-of-control world, and He will set you free as you walk out of the prison of a pressure cooker lifestyle.

Ponder and Practice

Now that we know how we can handle what we can't control, let's look at what we can control. What are some practical things you can start implementing into your life to reduce stress?

_____

_____

_____

_____

Here are a few practical tips we can try:

What are some things you can say no to?

_____

_____

_____

How can you manage busy days better?

_____

_____

_____

What are the sources of anxiety that you cannot control?

_____

_____

_____

Invite God to invade that prison. What can you control with some planning?

_____

_____

_____

How can you implement those plans into your daily life?

_____

_____

_____

How do you respond to stress, and how would you prefer to respond?

_____

_____

_____

Prayer

Lord God, we realize stress is a weapon of the enemy. Give us Your divine wisdom and discernment to change things up and make better decisions about our time and tasks. We can't control all our stress triggers, but You can when we invite You to invade our world. In Jesus's name. Amen.

DAY 30

God Commands Rest

He makes me to lie down in green pastures;
He leads me beside the still waters.

Psalm 23:2

WHEN MY DOCTOR RECOMMENDED I BEGIN TAKING NAPS, THE chains of guilt began breaking. In my mind, naps wasted time. I viewed any kind of inactivity as a lack of productivity. My slightly elevated blood pressure and itchy eczema clued my doctor in on my stress level.

The Ten Commandments don't preclude overworking, but they do include a day of rest to worship God. Our Creator knows the value of rest for our bodies to function well. God knows our needs better than we do. After all, He designed these intricate human machines.

In Psalm 23, the shepherd provides his sheep with a place conducive for rest. He works hard to provide green pastures for his flock. According to shepherd and pastor Phillip Keller, shepherds plant and irrigate the pastures, making them good grazing grounds for the sheep. The flock also won't settle down when they feel insecure, hungry, or fearful. The shepherd takes this into consideration when he prepares their serene pasture. Sheep cannot rest if they feel discomfort from flies aggravating them, so he anoints their heads with a special oil.[16]

A good shepherd provides a sense of safety for his flock. Does our Good Shepherd, Jesus Christ, do any less for us? When we give Him our schedules and our burdens, He allows us to rest.

The shepherd also leads his flock to the still waters to stay hydrated. Sheep won't drink from rushing water. Friend, we need to leave the rushing waters of the world behind and drink from the water of the Holy Spirit.

As a shepherd, David knew the needs of his father's flock. One night in the pastures, he probably began praying. He realized the similarities between his role as shepherd and the tender mercies of God. David has given us special insight into the role of shepherd in Psalm 23.

I discovered that when I allow God full reign over my life, I actually accomplish more. When I sit with God for an extended time praying and listening, I never fall behind.

God didn't create us to work like the Energizer Bunny or he would have included batteries. He wants us to be like the rabbits in my backyard, taking time as they nibble on clover. Your shepherd has prepared a time of rest for you. Will you take it?

Ponder and Practice

"It is vain for you to rise up early, to sit up late, to eat the bread of sorrow; for so He gives His beloved sleep" (Psalm 127:2). Ask the Holy Spirit to instruct you concerning stress and rest from this verse. What has He impressed upon you?

_____

_____

_____

What is your plan of action to obediently get more rest?

_____

_____

_____

What lies have you believed about rest?

_____

_____

_____

Remove the lies. Write out the truths you will use to replace the lies.

_____

_____

_____

"And He said to them, 'Come aside by yourselves to a deserted place and rest a while.' For there were many coming and going, and they did not even have time to eat" (Mark 6:31). What insight does this verse give you on your busiest days?

_____

_____

_____

Prayer

Lord Jesus, I'm sorry I haven't appreciated the rest You create for me with Your tender care. I haven't allowed You to rule over my schedule, but that changes today. I am setting that time aside now. Guard it from interruption and distraction. Thank You for being my Good Shepherd. Amen.

PART IV

Rejection and Fear

DAY 31

Wounded by Friendly Fire

Now Eliab his oldest brother heard when he spoke to the men;
and Eliab's anger was aroused against David, and he said, "Why
did you come down here? And with whom have you left those
few sheep in the wilderness? I know your pride and the inso-
lence of your heart, for you have come down to see the battle."

1 Samuel 17:28

NOTHING SCREAMS REJECTION MORE THAN FRIENDS PLANNING A
beach trip while they ensure you won't find out until they've safely
left town without you. Being uninvited stings, not like a honeybee but
rather like a scorpion. When I connected the dots of their deception,
my pain level rose to a ten.

At the request of his father, David left the sheep in someone
else's care while he delivered food to his brothers on the battle line.
When he arrived, David heard Goliath's threats against Israel. David
watched as his brothers and the entire Israelite army fled in fear.
Unafraid, David viewed Goliath as an uncircumcised Philistine who
defied the armies of the living God (1 Samuel 17:26).

David's oldest brother, Eliab, perceived that David considered
fighting Goliath. Enraged with jealousy, Eliab voiced false accusations
at David. He belittled his younger brother, accused him of neglect-
ing the sheep, and revealed the pride and the insolence of his heart.
According to *Strong's Concordance*, insolence means *evil*. The NIV
uses the word *wicked*.

As David considered fighting Goliath, a battle of words brewed. David felt the sting of rejection that we know so well. Eliab embarrassed his brother, hoping the army wouldn't see David's courage. But the Holy Spirit guided David. He didn't waste time arguing with Eliab. He had a bigger battle to fight.

Friend, I don't know how fresh your wounds are, but I'd love to respond to hurtful words and actions differently. David didn't ignore the painful remarks, but he chose not to surrender to them. God wants us to trust Him with our pain and rejection. If David could trust God while he fought a giant, he could trust God with his family's rejection.

Some people encourage us to be strong while others discourage us, making us even stronger.

David didn't allow his brother to interfere with God's calling on his life. We shouldn't allow the pain of rejection to stop us either. Let's trust God with our pain, refusing to give in to it. Instead, we can use it as a stepping-stone to serve God in giant ways.

Ponder and Practice
Which lies have you believed when you feel rejected?

_____

_____

_____

Place a check mark beside each one that applies.

Here are some truths to combat these lies. Look them up in your Bible and select the ones you want to keep handy to replace the lies the enemy whispers.

Jeremiah 31:3

1 Peter 3:3–4

John 10:10

1 Peter 4:12–13

Genesis 50:20

Which of these truths and the ones you have discovered yourself will you use to replace the lies?

_____

_____

_____

We don't need the world to validate our worth. God has already done that when He sacrificed His only Son so we can spend eternity with Him. What truths can you gather from that?

_____

_____

_____

Prayer

> *Lord God*, my heart aches because of the words people have said and the unkindness they have shown to me. Heal my wounds. I trust You with my pain, and I know it has happened for my good and Your glory. In Jesus's name. Amen.

DAY 32

Projecting Rejection

*And behold, a woman of Canaan came from that region and cried out to Him, saying, "Have mercy on me, O Lord, Son of David! My daughter is severely demon-possessed."
But He answered her not a word.
And His disciples came and urged Him, saying, "Send her away, for she cries out after us."*

Matthew 15:22–23

I ANTICIPATED THE RIDICULE WHICH BEGAN WHEN MY CLASSMATES realized their team was stuck with me. If I had collapsed in a heap of tears, would they have excused me from gym class? Instead, I stuffed it down. Why didn't anyone understand the humiliation I bore as a legally blind child?

Jesus traveled into the coastal region where a gentile woman approached Him. She cried out wanting Jesus to make her daughter whole.

Jesus remained silent, but her continual cries annoyed His disciples. They implored Jesus, "Send her away!" With the disciples sounding like my classmates, I would have bolted. But not our sister. She knew Jesus as her compassionate Lord. Counting on His kindness, she reasoned with Jesus.

Then Jesus said something that sounded harsh. "It is not good to take the children's bread and throw it to the little dogs" (Matthew 15:26). The Greek term translated *little dogs* refers to little house pets, not wild scavengers as it does elsewhere in Scripture.

In humility, our Canaanite sister replied, "The little dogs eat the crumbs which fall from their masters' table" (Matthew 15:27). She understood Jesus's earthly ministry belonged to Israel, but she wanted a few crumbs from her Master's hand.

Despite the shunning from the disciples and an indefinite answer from Jesus, she persisted. Perhaps she'd grown accustomed to the slurs of sailors who docked their ships in that port.

Jesus rewarded her steadfastness: "Great is your faith" (Matthew 15:28). And He healed her daughter.

My childhood rejection carried over into my adult years. For decades, I lacked the courage to ask anyone for help. I listened to the lies Satan fed me: *You're a burden. You are different, and that's unacceptable.* Then I realized what this woman already knew—Jesus loves and accepts me, and that's enough.

Have you felt cast aside? Has someone in your past planted seeds of humiliation?

A woman of faith clothes herself in humility, not humiliation.

Refuse to live under the lies of Satan. See yourself through the eyes of Jesus, beloved and accepted.

Ponder and Practice

Jesus didn't reject this woman, but sometimes we project rejection on ourselves, taking something the wrong way. For example, Jesus's comment about little dogs could have been interpreted as an insult. I know I am guilty of this at times. Past hurts can make us hypersensitive to comments that aren't intended to hurt us. When have you projected rejection on yourself when it might not have been intended that way?

_____

_____

_____

What lies did Satan cause you to believe in the past? How did they carry over into your adult years?

_____

_____

_____

How can trusting in the love and acceptance of Jesus help you see yourself through His eyes and not through the lens of rejection?

_____

_____

_____

Read the entire passage in Matthew 15:21–28. Can you identify the six pieces of God's armor this woman used? Write them down in the appropriate places. How can you use these to prevent yourself from projecting rejection?

Belt of truth:

_____

_____

Breastplate of righteousness:

_____

_____

Shoes of peace:

_____

_____

Helmet of salvation:

_____

_____

Shield of faith:

_____

_____

Sword of the Spirit:

_____

_____

Prayer

> *Lord Jesus*, thank You for Your love and acceptance. You've helped me realize I'm worthy. Help me not fall prey to more hurt by projecting rejection when it's not real. In Jesus's name. Amen.

DAY 33

My Need to Feel Needed

That Christ may dwell in your hearts through faith; that you,
being rooted and grounded in love, may be able to comprehend
with all the saints what is the width and length and depth and
height—to know the love of Christ which passes knowledge.

Ephesians 3:17–19

"HELLO?" NO RESPONSE. EVERYONE HAD GONE TO THEIR GROUPS,
leaving me alone. Immediately, I traveled back in time to that middle-
school girl alone on the playground. *Snap out of it, Carolyn! Your*
computer malfunction left you in the Zoom meeting alone. A phone
call to the tech person placed me in a breakout room with people
happy to see me.

Isn't it strange how something so insignificant can send us into
yesteryear, feeling discarded? I think that friendless little girl will
always exist down deep inside, along with a teenager desperate for
acceptance. Like a curse that follows us through time, the wound that
comes from being excluded continues to reopen. That old familiar
pain resurfaces, and vulnerability settles in.

Friend, I have felt your heartache. I have walked a similar path. If
we could sit in the same room, I'd give you a hug. We can't continue
reopening that wound each time someone snubs us. How do we break
that cycle?

We turn to Jesus, who knows rejection, but He will never reject us. Today's verses tell us He wants to dwell in our hearts. That doesn't mean He wants to drop in for a visit. He wants to hang out, but do we hang out with Jesus? When we dwell with Him, His love stabilizes us. Paul used the term *rooted*, like the deep roots of a tree that has withstood years of storms. *Grounded* refers to a solid foundation that doesn't crumble with time. The love of Christ secures us when people stir up insecurities.

Friend, I've found I must turn to Jesus when I'm uninvited elsewhere. He invites me in with open arms full of love. And that's the next thing Paul penned: "To know the love of Christ which passes knowledge; that you may be filled with all the fullness of God" (Ephesians 3:19).

When we make time for Christ, He fills us with His immeasurable love. Then we can pour that love out on others, instead of expecting them to fill the love void in our hearts.

My need to feel needed can only be filled by Jesus.

Ponder and Practice

Today's Scriptures come from one of Paul's prayers that focuses on enabling Christians to live the Spirit-filled life. We have to stop when we see the flesh taking control—and it can happen just as quickly as it did that day on my computer. When that happens and we stand face-to-face with rejection, what choice must we face?

_____

_____

_____

Pay attention to the words *rooted*, *grounded*, and *steadfast* as you reread today's verses. Now read Colossians 2:5–10. What do these verses say about a stable faith—one that is rooted and grounded?

_____

_____

_____

Look at verse 8. How can human tradition cheat us?

_____

_____

_____

What is a spiritual way you can respond to rejection?

_____

_____

_____

How are we made complete (verse 10)?

_____

_____

_____

Prayer

Heavenly Father, when I feel the familiar sting of rejection, help me respond in the Spirit and not in the flesh. Heal my heart from both past and present wounds. Help me live in the knowledge that I am complete in You. In Jesus's name. Amen.

DAY 34

God Meets Us

*Now the Angel of the Lord found her by a spring of water
in the wilderness, by the spring on the way to Shur.*

Genesis 16:7

"HEY, LADY, THERE'S A BEAR!"

Jumping with a frightful scream, I annoyed the black bear, and
he let out a terrifying growl, shaking me to the core.

"Where is he?" I was unable to see the bear, so my instincts kicked
in, seeking answers.

With a hint of disappointment, the man on the balcony answered,
"He's gone back into the woods."

Black bears frequently roam throughout Gatlinburg, Tennessee,
despite the numerous tourists. My first encounter left me trembling,
but I knew God intervened.

Sarai, Abram's wife, couldn't conceive children. This occurred
before God changed their names to Sarah and Abraham. Sarai took
matters into her own hands when she told Abram to have children
with her maid, Hagar. After Hagar became pregnant, the relationship
between the two women grew bitter. Sarai dealt harshly with Hagar.

Hagar refused to continue being mistreated, so she fled. Hagar
fled rejection, but she ran right into fear. How could a pregnant
woman survive in the wilderness alone?

Today's verse tells us the Angel of the Lord found Hagar. The term *Angel of the Lord* here refers to a pre-incarnate presence of Jesus Christ. Jesus met her in the midst of her brokenness.

Friend, I want to encourage you that He meets us too. Today, your heart might ache from someone's unkindness. You might face life with dread. Possibly, you fear what God has called you to do because you can't handle it if someone rejects you.

Hagar felt so unwanted and unloved after Sarai and Abram had used her, but God met her. God meets us in our wilderness.

I felt alone with that bear, just Iva and me. The guy on the balcony couldn't stop the bear, but God met me.

Whatever you face today, God will meet you right in the middle of it all. Maybe you look back at something in retrospect. Like me, you ask, *Where was God?* We'd prefer for certain situations to never happen, but it gives God the opportunity to meet us when we need Him most.

That's what I want you to take away from today's message. I want you to remember Hagar, alone and afraid. When you feel frightened and left out, remember the Angel of the Lord met Hagar, and He will meet you too.

Ponder and Practice

Throughout the Bible, God meets people in their most vulnerable moments. Read this passage.

> And they heard the sound of the LORD God walking in the garden in the cool of the day, and Adam and his wife hid themselves from the presence of the LORD God among the trees of the garden. Then the LORD God called to Adam and said to him, "Where are you?" (Genesis 3:8–9)

In what situation did God meet Adam?

_____

_____

Read Daniel 3:14–25. The three Hebrews demonstrated bravery. How do you think they felt?

_____

_____

Where did the Lord meet them?

_____

_____

When Paul journeyed on a ship headed to Rome, a fierce storm interrupted their trip. They threw the ship's tackle overboard to prevent sinking. Read Acts 27:22–24. How did God encourage Paul?

_____

_____

_____

Describe a time when God has met you in your wilderness, the fiery furnace, or even in a terrifying storm.

_____

_____

_____

Prayer

Lord Jesus, thank You for never leaving me and always meeting me when I need You most. Help me not be afraid because You are with me. Amen.

DAY 35

Where Does Fear Come From?

*For God has not given us a spirit of fear, but of
power and of love and of a sound mind.*

2 Timothy 1:7

I HEARD THE ENEMY'S FAMILIAR HISS AS I FOLDED THE LAST SHIRT, happy with my selections. *What are you thinking, going on a ministry retreat with strangers? They won't help you. You'll go hungry, and you won't find a bathroom either.*

Finding bathrooms and food occupied the top of my need-to-know list when Timmy didn't accompany me. I seldom went anywhere without him. Without sight, these things panicked me, and the enemy knew it. Even now, he tries pushing those buttons.

Fear didn't exist in the garden of Eden until Adam and Eve sinned. Immediately, shame came on the scene. Then, when God walked in the garden, fear made its grand entrance as Adam and Eve tried to hide. Their sin and shame created apprehension, and it's plagued us ever since.

In today's verse, Paul told Timothy God doesn't give us the spirit of fear. Since fear originated from sin, it comes from the enemy.

Paul continued instructing Timothy about this dreadful emotion, which in the Greek connotes cowardice. God had called Timothy to preach, and with that call, He empowered Timothy with the Holy Spirit. Whatever God has called you to do, He has provided you the power you'll need to accomplish it. Perhaps it includes writing, teaching Sunday school, or even a secular job.

The Holy Spirit also gives us love for lost souls. Have you wondered how missionaries can surrender their lives, taking risks to serve in foreign countries? God gives us the love to see people saved.

God also gives us self-control—a sensible head. When we renew our minds, God keeps us balanced.

Fear says, *You can't*. Faith says, *I will*.

With the authority of Christ and the power of the Holy Spirit, we can stand our ground, defending our faith from the slimy, tampering claws of the devil. That's what I did that day as I packed for my trip. I never went without food or a bathroom. The experience increased my faith.

We learn to recognize the enemy's voice and his familiar lies. But sweet friend, we've also learned how to replace those lies with God's truth. When fear comes knocking on your door, heed the warning. Use the Word of God to usher him from your presence.

Ponder and Practice

What makes you afraid?

_____

_____

_____

Today's passage says God gives us power. How have you seen the Spirit's power help you, especially in overcoming fear?

_____

_____

_____

How can love overpower fear?

_____

_____

_____

Have you noticed a more balanced or stable foundation in your life now when you compare today with your thoughts and mindset five years ago?

_____

_____

_____

"Fear not, for I am with you; be not dismayed, for I am your God. I will strengthen you, yes, I will help you, I will uphold you with My righteous right hand" (Isaiah 41:10).

List the reasons this verse gives you not to fear.

_____

_____

_____

How can you apply God's Word to your fears?

_____

_____

_____

We've covered much territory today, but until we implement what we learn, it cannot help us. What is one thing you can change right now to address your fears with faith?

_____

_____

_____

What do you need to ask God to help you with concerning fear?

_____

_____

_____

Prayer

Heavenly Father, I realize fear doesn't come from You. When I feel afraid, I recognize the enemy. Help me depend on Your power, love, and a sound mind to eradicate fear in my life. In Jesus's name. Amen.

DAY 36

How the Enemy Uses Fear

When Saul and all Israel heard these words of the Philistine, they were dismayed and greatly afraid.

1 Samuel 17:11

EXHILARATION FLOWED THROUGH MY VEINS AS WE ARRIVED AT the hotel for my writing retreat. I planned ten days of praying, fasting, and writing, just Iva and me in Gatlinburg, but would the bears send me home early, especially after the last encounter? Would my old foe, fear, bring my unpacking to a halt?

"Don't go outside alone," warned the desk clerk.

I looked at Timmy, who planned to return home the next day. I explained our plans to the desk clerk, assuring her we'd done this before. She gave another stern warning. With her optimism, how did this hotel keep any guests?

I began putting my clothes in the drawers as apprehension overwhelmed me. Hadn't I conquered fear before? Would Iva and I be safe?

We went to the store, and I stayed in the car. I began praying, and I found a website with verses about fear. I sat in that parking lot, and I repeated each verse out loud. I felt the power of God's Word as His peace overcame me. Without realizing it, I had replaced fear's lies with the truth.

Goliath sounded an alarming terror for the entire Israelite army, including King Saul. Why did they cower in fear when David had the courage to fight Goliath? Saul exhibited some spiritual problems, and he didn't have a tight relationship with God like David.

The further we are from God, the closer we are to fear.

The enemy uses this tactic to intimidate us in hopes we either back down or fight from a place of cowardice instead of victory. But when we stay close to God, He covers us in His perfect love which casts out fear (1 John 4:18). When we possess a mature love for God, we don't have to fear the worst judgment of all—the wrath of God. When we know God has rescued us from that torment, our boldness should cause us to walk in faith, not trembling.

Fear is the thermostat by which we can measure our proximity to God.

The bear came visiting as we sat on our second-floor balcony. He amused Iva when he walked past us and destroyed a grill on the patio below. God prevailed.

The enemy will use our qualms to cause us to fight from the point of fear or not even show up to fight at all. What response will you choose today? I encourage you to trust God with your fears. The victory has been won.

Ponder and Practice
How were David and King Saul different? Which one do you most identify with?

_____

_____

_____

How does a close relationship with God put distance between us and fear?

_____

_____

_____

In what way(s) would you like your relationship with God to change?

_____

_____

_____

How do you plan to implement these changes?

_____

_____

_____

Without a plan, we will only drift farther from God, not closer. When we set these types of goals, we must expect enemy interference. He doesn't want God's daughters drawing closer to the Lord.

"I sought the Lord, and He heard me, and delivered me from all my fears" (Psalm 34:4). Pray over this verse and write down what God reveals to you.

_____

_____

_____

What giants do you face today? Do you fight from a point of fear or a point of victory?

_____

_____

_____

Prayer

Lord Jesus, I want the courage of David, and I desire to draw closer to You each day. Set a hedge of protection around our time together. In Jesus's name. Amen.

DAY 37

Do You Dread Change?

You prepare a table before me in the presence of my enemies.
Psalm 23:5

I HAVE A LOT IN COMMON WITH SHEEP. THEY HAVE LOW VISION, and they don't like change. Whether it's the new setup at Walmart, new seating at church, or all things COVID, change brings challenges. New surroundings stir up angst for me, just like the thought of retirement may stir up insecurities for others.

Since shepherds move their sheep from pasture to pasture and from the valley to the high country, how can they calm the sheep's apprehension to change? Can we depend on our Good Shepherd to calm our foreboding hearts about the changes happening in our lives?

A shepherd takes his sheep to the high country, known as the tableland, every summer. He goes before his flock preparing the plateau for them. He removes poisonous plants, leaving salt and minerals for his flock. He cleans out the water sources. Despite his efforts, the shepherd cannot remove all dangers.[17]

Cougars can hide and pounce upon a straying sheep. If the shepherd can deliver that sheep from the enemy, the sheep learns staying near the shepherd provides security. The flock soon learns they have no reason to fear in the presence of the shepherd.

Jesus goes before us, removing the toxins of this world. He doesn't want us drinking from polluted waters when He offers us the refreshing water of the Word that sanctifies us.

Whether you dread new procedures at work or have misgivings about a major life change such as retirement or rehabbing after surgery, intimacy with our Good Shepherd plays a vital role in a peaceful transition. Consider all the steps a shepherd takes to protect his flock, creating a calm atmosphere for them. Will Jesus do any less for us?

I'll still do an eye roll when updates occur on my computer or smartphone, and I prefer not to think about major life changes. Can we commit to remind ourselves that Jesus has worked to provide us a stable transition?

I have peace about tomorrow because God's been there today. No matter if that tomorrow holds a layoff, a life-altering illness, a new phase in life, or just a frustrating rearrangement at the store, God has prepared tomorrow for us.

Ponder and Practice

Read the first two chapters of Nehemiah. After seventy years in captivity, some Jews made the journey back to Judah and found the walls broken down. How do you think the Jews felt about the changes in their lives?

_____

_____

_____

How did Nehemiah prepare for the new task facing him?

_____

_____

_____

When facing an impending change in your life, like a new job or a move, do you pray and fast?

Four months passed between Nehemiah chapters 1 and 2. How do you handle waiting on answer to prayer for that long?

_____

_____

_____

I don't wait well, especially with something as disheartening as the ruins of Nehemiah's beloved homeland must have been. How do you think God worked when it appeared nothing at all was happening?

_____

_____

_____

I love the way God worked on the secular king in a secular government to provide Nehemiah with more than he imagined. What gives you hope when you cannot see God at work?

_____

_____

_____

Prayer

> *Lord Jesus*, when life changes, I can cancel out the dread and apprehension I feel by drawing closer to You like the sheep drawing nigh to their shepherd. I can exemplify Nehemiah's pattern of prayer and fasting, trusting You are working. Amen.

DAY 38

When Jesus Calls Us Out of the Boat

And Peter answered Him and said, "Lord, if it is You,
command me to come to You on the water."
Matthew 14:28

YOU HOLD THIS BOOK IN YOUR HANDS BECAUSE JESUS CALLED ME onto the waves. Leaving the security of working with a dear Christian publisher to work with a faith-filled team of Christian sisters at Redemption Press required a huge investment—one that risked triggering a tsunami of events.

Jesus urged His disciples to get into the boat, promising to meet them on the other side. During their nighttime journey, they sailed into a fierce storm. Jesus went to them walking on the storm-tossed sea. The disciples grew more fearful of this ghostly figure on the water than of the storm itself.

Then Jesus spoke the same words He speaks to me. They're the same words He speaks to you: "Do not be afraid" (Matthew 14:27).

Overwhelmed by the sight of Jesus walking toward them, presumptuous Peter asked Jesus to command him to join Him. Peter desired to share an amazing experience with His Lord. His courage soared thinking about the feel of the water under his feet.

Jesus said, "Come" (Matthew 14:29).

Ecstatic, Peter rushed to climb out of the boat. Eyes locked on Jesus, Peter took one step and then another. He did it! He walked on the stormy waves. Eyes of faith find security in the eyes of Jesus.

Then the whipping winds caught Peter's attention, drawing his focus from Jesus to the storm. Trembling, Peter began sinking. "Lord, save me!" (Matthew 14:30).

Immediately, Jesus caught Peter, and He asked, "Why did you doubt?" (Matthew 14:31).

Like Peter, I signed my publishing contract with exuberance, but the winds of fear might blow in one day. At that time, I hope I'll be grounded enough not to remove my eyes from Jesus, and I won't allow doubt and anxiety to pull me under.

Friend, has God called you out onto the water? Trust Jesus to rescue you when the winds and waves surround you with fearful lies. When we lose our balance, we must trust Him to give us His hand. He has rescued us from hell, and He will rescue us from the storms that frighten us. Can you say yes to Jesus today?

Ponder and Practice

What Bible truth do you turn to when you feel afraid? That is your belt of truth.

_____

_____

_____

Find one more verse to conquer your doubts and fears to use as the sword of the Spirit, something you can wound the enemy with.

_____

_____

_____

While we live in the flesh, it wars with the Spirit. We don't trust in our own righteousness, but in the righteousness of Christ. It's His breastplate we wear. The enemy wants us to feel unworthy. What does Job 29:14 say about righteousness?

_____

_____

_____

Read John 16:33 and Psalm 56:3. How will you put on the shoes of peace in the storms of fear?

_____

_____

_____

Jesus has given us the authority to lift up the shield of faith against the enemy. Choose one verse that encourages you to fully trust God and hold up your shield.

_____

_____

_____

Terrifying thoughts trickle into our minds unless we wear the helmet of salvation. What thoughts make you afraid?

_____

_____

_____

Create a plan to take those thoughts captive and remove them.

_____

_____

_____

Prayer

Lord Jesus, clothe me in Your righteousness. Fear doesn't come from You but from the enemy. Help me memorize verses I can recall when those thoughts threaten to invade my mind and my peace. You are my peace. In Jesus's name. Amen.

DAY 39

No Condemnation

But immediately Jesus spoke to them, saying, "Be
of good cheer! It is I; do not be afraid."

Matthew 14:27

THE DOG RELEASED A FEROCIOUS BARK AS HE SPED OUT THE DOOR,
racing toward us. I knew a fence separated us, but despite Iva's high
level of intelligence, she responded like a dog who had been attacked
by dogs before.

Frightened, Iva picked up her pace, almost running. Within
seconds, she realized she was still guiding me, as she slowed down
to a normal speed. When some distance separated us from the barking dog, I stopped. Iva's response conveyed despair. My heart broke
when I realized Iva's fear of this dog. Kneeling beside her, I rubbed
her velvety black ears. "You're okay."

As I picked up the harness and we began walking, God trans-
ported me to the Sea of Galilee when Jesus said, "Be of good cheer! It
is I; do not be afraid" (Matthew 14:27).

As Jesus approached the ship, walking on the water, He saw the
fear on the faces of His disciples. He knew their terrified thoughts.
When He encouraged them, reassuring them of His presence, He
didn't speak in a harsh tone of condemnation. He spoke the words
in loving comfort, like I spoke to Iva.

Jesus understood then and He understands now why certain
things will always cause us to tremble. He wants to remove our fears.

He knows when danger exists and when it doesn't, just like I knew the dog couldn't reach us.

Friend, I don't know what things make you apprehensive. Has a past incident created some angst for you? Do reminders of some horrific event still haunt you?

God has a loving nature. As our Father, He wants our unwavering faith, but sometimes that seems impossible to give. Barking dogs arouse Iva's fear. The thought of having COVID again causes me to have a hypersensitivity toward safety. Each of us has weaknesses, but God doesn't disdain our insecurity.

Our fears arouse compassion in Christ, not condemnation. Jesus never condemns us. Instead, His compassionate heart aches for us because we shouldn't be afraid. He aches because we fail to trust Him.

Friend, perhaps certain situations cause your heart to race a little harder. Know that the Lord understands your fear, and He stands by your side, ready to help you conquer it.

Ponder and Practice

What is that one thing your faith hasn't conquered yet?

_____

_____

_____

How do you think Jesus feels about that fear you haven't overcome?

_____

_____

_____

What other feelings accompany that emotion of fear?

_____

_____

_____

How do you feel about yourself, that fear, and other emotions?

_____

_____

_____

Using your answers above, what lies do you believe?

_____

_____

_____

Which truths will you choose to replace the lies? Here are some options: Isaiah 41:10; John 14:27; Colossians 2:10; or 1 John 4:4.

_____

_____

_____

Prayer

Lord, You encourage me when I'm afraid. Your peace exceeds all my fears. You never condemn me when life grows distressful. I know when I am afraid, You are with me, and I have no reason to fear. In Jesus's name. Amen.

DAY 40

Who Rules?

You shall not be afraid of the terror by night,
Nor of the arrow that flies by day,
Nor of the pestilence that walks in darkness,
Nor of the destruction that lays waste at noonday.

Psalm 91:5–6

IVA INCREASED HER PACE AS WE WALKED ALONG THE WOODS ENJOY-ing the shady trees. Was she rushing to greet a friend ahead of us?

"Wait, Iva." I slowed her down. "Hello?" It sounded more like a question than a greeting.

A hideous growl broke the peaceful melody of singing birds. Unable to see this growling creature, I feared the worst. Was it a coyote? Some had been spotted in this area. Another bear, or perhaps a loose dog? I grabbed my personal alarm as its shrill decibels rang throughout our neighborhood, and step by step, I backed away afraid to turn around.

Seconds passed like hours until someone came to our rescue. My neighbor discovered a pit bull running loose in the woods, and he escorted us past the danger.

Have you faced some terrifying event or predator? One moment in time turns into horror. Psalm 91 encourages us not to allow fear to reign in our lives. It gives us two reasons.

First, look at who our God is, our *refuge* and *fortress* (Psalm 91:2).

Next, we don't allow fear to control us because of what God does: "Surely, He shall deliver you from the snare of the fowler and from the perilous pestilence" (Psalm 91:3). This verbiage connotes a hunter's trap for animals and also disease. COVID has dictated our lives for far too long.

"He shall cover you with His feathers, and under His wings you shall take refuge" (Psalm 91:4). The image of a mother hen fluffing out her wings to hide her baby chicks from the chicken hawk swooping down at them paints a portrait of intimacy.

With all these pictures of protection, why do bad things still happen?

We see this passage through worldly eyes and not eyes of faith. We want health, healing, and safety, but we forget these dire situations are momentary afflictions compared to the glory to come (Romans 8:18). We tend to be so earthly minded we forget the heavenly perspective.

We can't allow fear to rule over us. Instead, let's trust our Father even when we don't understand.

Ponder and Practice

"He who dwells in the secret place of the Most High shall abide under the shadow of the Almighty" (Psalm 91:1) The promises we want to cling to have a condition: a personal, abiding relationship with the Lord. We can't expect God to cover us when we have a long-distance relationship with Him.

What conditions do you find in verses 1 and 9 of Psalm 91?

_____

_____

_____

What changes can you make to have more intimacy with God?

_____

_____

_____

What fears control you? How can you use this passage to address those particular fears today?

_____

_____

_____

Verse 4 describes the truth of God. The shield was large enough to cover one person, just like the Roman shield Paul referred to as our shield of faith in the New Testament. The buckler is a mound of earth that surrounds a fortress. What does this tell you about your situation?

_____

_____

_____

Look up verse 4 in several different translations. What are some of the ways His truth is described here?

_____

_____

_____

Prayer

> _Lord God_, I face this fear. Break me free from its control over me. Help me draw closer to You and completely trust You even when I don't understand what You are doing. In Jesus's name. Amen.

PART V

Anger, Bitterness, Unforgiveness, and Shame

DAY 41

The Danger of Anger

If you do well, will you not be accepted? And if you do not do well, sin lies at the door. And its desire is for you, but you should rule over it."

Genesis 4:7

DO YOU STRUGGLE WITH ANGER? I CONFESS I DO. ANGER ISN'T sinful. God gets angry, but anger, even righteous indignation, can lead to sin. It provoked the first murder when Cain killed his brother, Abel, but did you know God gave Cain an escape?

As we unpack Genesis chapter 4, we will discover how we can take the escape Cain refused. Cain brought an offering from the fruit of the ground, but Abel brought of the firstborn of his flock. The Lord respected Abel's offering, but not Cain's (Genesis 4:3–5).

Why didn't God accept Cain's offering? God revealed what He wanted in an offering, although Scripture doesn't tell us. He wanted a blood sacrifice and an obedient heart. Cain ignored God's instructions. Cain's flesh ruled him, and a fierce anger kindled in him when God rejected his inappropriate offering.

God questioned Cain, "Why are you angry? And why has your countenance fallen?" (Genesis 4:6).

Then God gave Cain two choices with polar opposite outcomes. Cain could do well, bring the appropriate offering, and God would accept him. His other choice included continuing in the temptation and eventual sin. God gave Cain a second chance. God warned him about the sin waiting at the door and its desire for him.

God told Cain to rule over the sin. Cain possessed that authority like we do. Rule over sin before sin rules over you.

God gave Cain an escape from the sin crouching at the door, waiting to pounce on him, but Cain gave in to the devil's temptation. Satan pushes those buttons creating anger, grudges, and bitterness because he seeks to destroy us (John 10:10).

God gives us options just as he gave Cain options. How can we rule over anger that leads to sin (Psalm 4:4)?

We choose whether or not to act on the rage building inside us. When we turn to the Bible, God's power can overcome our flesh, including our anger.

I've learned to let go, shut my mouth, and take God's escape route. When sin rules over us, we gratify the flesh and grieve the Spirit. If anger tempts you, look for God's exit.

Ponder and Practice

"We should love one another, not as Cain who was of the wicked one and murdered his brother. And why did he murder him? Because his works were evil and his brother's righteous" (1 John 3:11–12).

How could Cain escape the anger before it became the sin of murder?

_____

_____

_____

What makes you angry?

_____

_____

How do you handle it?

_____

_____

_____

Think about a time when you grew angry. What escape could you have taken? Did you take the escape route God provided?

_____

_____

_____

Cain's countenance also fell. That tells us he not only had a fierce anger raging within, but he also had to deal with feelings of rejection and anxiety.

Let's write out the three Rs for Cain. What lie did he believe?

_____

_____

_____

What truth could have helped him or could help you?

_____

_____

_____

Prayer

Lord God, help me rule over my anger and bitterness. I want to take Your way of escape. Help me not bear a grudge either. In Jesus's name. Amen.

DAY 42

Avoiding the Root of Bitterness

Let all bitterness, wrath, anger, clamor, and evil speak-
ing be put away from you, with all malice.

Ephesians 4:31

WHEN YOU CUT DOWN POISON HEMLOCK, YOU SCATTER THE SEEDS
for the next crop. With its adverse side effects, you don't want it grow-
ing in your backyard. When you come in contact with it, you may
experience an itchy rash, as if you got into some poison ivy, but if
ingested, poison hemlock can prove fatal. You must dig up the root to
kill this fast-spreading toxin. Likewise, we must take prompt action
to remove anger from our hearts before the sun goes down on our
wrath. Anger unchecked takes root as bitterness.

Years passed as I tried removing bitterness. As soon as I felt I had
succeeded, the same person hurt me or a loved one again. This continued for years. The enemy had trapped me in a prison, and I wanted out.

When we allow anger to feel at home in our hearts, we risk grow-
ing bitter. God tells us to put off the old man (Ephesians 4:22) and
be renewed in the spirit of the mind (Ephesians 4:23). I wanted to
forgive. I didn't like the bitterness that rose up each time I heard the
name of the person who hurt me. While I asked Jesus to remove every
root of bitterness, the devil continued fanning the flames of anger. If
this person who wounded me and my loved ones could stop hurting
people, I could make progress.

Have you been there, my friend? Someone continues to reopen unhealed wounds, and you pay the price as you sit in the prison of bitterness.

God warns us not to give place to the devil (Ephesians 4:27). Don't grieve the Holy Spirit (Ephesians 4:30). Each time she wronged someone, I gave in to the devil. I'd call a friend and rant about her evil deeds. No wonder I couldn't find joy. I continued to grieve the Holy Spirit. It took a long time, but I have finally broken free from the bondage of bitterness.

I'm better when I'm not bitter.

If you can identify with my ordeal, I want you to know you can destroy that bitterness, even though it may be difficult. You can do it.

Now that we understand how offensive bitterness is to the Holy Spirit and ourselves, we must be intentional about removing wrath before it establishes a root in our hearts.

Ponder and Practice

Bitterness, which is unforgiveness, never hurts the person we can't forgive. It hurts us. It holds us hostage to the pain they inflicted on us. When we hold a grudge, we allow one hurtful incident to continue inflicting pain on us multiple times. We—not they—hold the key to release ourselves from this prison.

What root of bitterness have you not released?

_____

_____

_____

When you become angry, how difficult is it to let go of it before the sun goes down on your wrath?

_____

_____

_____

How do you handle people who hurt you?

_____

_____

_____

For someone who has wounded your heart multiple times, make a list of each incident. Ask God to help you forgive and not continue in bitterness with each individual offense.

We can't control the actions of others, but we can control our response. That includes taking our thoughts captive, removing them, and replacing them with truth.

What are three Rs you can use for this person who has hurt you?

_____

_____

_____

Prayer

Lord Jesus, I know people hurt You and betrayed You when You walked as a man. You know exactly how I feel. Please cleanse me of all anger, bitterness, and unforgiveness. Help me walk with a renewed mind. Amen.

DAY 43

The Best of Ruth and the Bitterness of Naomi

*But she said to them, "Do not call me Naomi; call me
Mara, for the Almighty has dealt very bitterly with me."*

Ruth 1:20

I NEVER IMAGINED GOD WOULD ALLOW ME TO LOSE MY HEARING,
the sense I depend on most since I'm blind. I didn't blame God, but
I resented the doctors who wasted my window of opportunity for
recovery, a term I soon heard often.

In 2019, I lost a dramatic amount of hearing within a split second
while sitting in my quiet living room. Multiple trips to multiple
doctors left me frustrated and upset.

After six weeks, I visited a specialist who diagnosed me with
Sudden Sensory Neuro Hearing Loss. I had missed the window of
opportunity since the condition needed to be treated as an emergency.

As the doctors expected, all treatments failed to restore any
hearing, but God restored it six months later. Bitterness toward the
doctors, especially my primary care physician, remained months after
the miracle.

Naomi's husband suggested packing up the boys and leaving the
famine in Bethlehem for the foreign country of Moab even though

it displeased God. They sought life and food, but soon all three men died. Naomi didn't rush back home. But when she heard Bethlehem had an abundance of food, she returned with Ruth, her loyal daughter-in-law who sought to know God.

Upon their arrival, the local women came out to meet Naomi. They saw the stress etched on her face. Naomi means pleasant, and with a quick snap, she requested the people call her Mara, meaning bitter.

Ruth responded to her husband's death and her subsequent poverty in faith, but Naomi resented God because He had afflicted her (Ruth 1:21).

During harvesttime, Ruth and Boaz married and had a son, whom Naomi loved. God had to break Naomi's resentfulness in order to make her a blessed joy-filled woman. Naomi proves hope exists for the bitter heart.

The breaking of me will be the making of me. "God doesn't have it out for you. He's looking out for you" (Liz Curtis Higgs).[18]

After several months and endless prayers, my grudge against the doctors disappeared. Friend, we lose seasons of joy while resentment reigns. Let's focus on God, living the best life like Ruth instead of the bitter life of Naomi.

Ponder and Practice

In which circumstances do you feel resentful, bitter, or afflicted by God? Why?

———————————————————————————

———————————————————————————

———————————————————————————

Naomi didn't appreciate Ruth. Which blessings have you not appreciated?

———————————————————————————

———————————————————————————

———————————————————————————

Let's dress Naomi in God's armor, and you can return here when you feel bitterness taking root in your life.

Belt of truth: What truth from Scripture reminds you that you can respond like Ruth and not Naomi (Options include: Philippians 4:13; 2 Corinthians 12:9)?

_____

_____

Breastplate of righteousness: We are clothed in the righteousness of Christ. What does Romans 1:17 say to you?

_____

_____

Shoes of peace: How does Philippians 4:6–7 apply to you today?

_____

_____

Shield of faith: Search for Bible verses about faith and find a verse that reminds you to trust God to quench the fiery arrows of the evil one. Write your favorite here:

_____

_____

Helmet of salvation: The mind is a battlefield. Choose Philippians 4:8, Colossians 3:2, or a favorite of your choice. Write it here.

_____

_____

What is your sword of the Spirit?

_____

_____

Prayer

Lord, dress me in Your armor so I don't have to live the bitter life of Naomi. With You I can live the better life of Ruth. In Jesus's name. Amen.

DAY 44

God Meant Good

But as for you, you meant evil against me; but God meant it for good,
in order to bring it about as it is this day, to save many people alive.

Genesis 50:20

BEAUTY AROSE OUT OF THE ASHES OF MY HEARING LOSS. I WITNESSED God's miraculous healing after doctors exhausted all possible cures, and I discovered the beauty in waiting on God. Still, the dark cloud of unforgiveness followed me for several months before I could in all honesty feel no lingering grudge against the doctors.

Do you recall Joseph's story? His jealous brothers plotted to kill him, but they sold him into slavery instead. His master's wife wrongly accused Joseph of raping her, so his master threw him into an Egyptian prison, where he dwelled forgotten and alone. When Pharaoh had some mysterious dreams no one could explain, a former prisoner remembered Joseph, the interpreter of dreams. Pharaoh called Joseph before him and made Joseph second in command under him to carry out a plan to store grain for seven upcoming years of famine.

When his brothers showed up in Egypt searching for food, they eventually reunited Joseph with his father, and they all lived in Egypt. But when their father died, his brothers feared Joseph because of the evil they had done.

God's good will always surpass Satan's evil.

Joseph knew he had to forgive them because God had shown him favor and used their evil to bring about good. When Joseph interpreted Pharaoh's dreams, it allowed him to develop a plan to collect plenty of food, which kept many people alive during the famine.

Joseph viewed his brothers' evil plot through eyes of faith. Their outrageous acts deserved God's wrath rather than mercy, but Joseph wasn't God, and neither are we. My friend, we must always seek the good God will bring out of a man's wrongdoing. Here's where it gets difficult—even when we don't see the good, we must trust God to work all things together for good (Romans 8:28).

Does God expect us to forgive some horrific offense? No, not on our own. He wants to help us forgive. Let's take one step and choose forgiveness, and God will meet us, leading us the rest of the way.

Ponder and Practice
Unforgiveness always holds us hostage to our past. Who needs your forgiveness?

_____

_____

How does this unforgiveness hold you hostage to your past?

_____

_____

_____

How does it interfere with your life?

_____

_____

_____

How does your unforgiveness hurt the person you need to forgive?

_____

_____

_____

In most cases, it doesn't hurt them at all. It always comes back on us. With unforgiveness, what we believe might not be all lies. For example, in Joseph's case, his brothers had plotted to murder him until God intervened with the traveling Ishmaelites. That is not a lie. What lies do you need to replace with the truth of today's verse?

_____

_____

_____

What are the facts?

_____

_____

How can today's verse and Joseph's story give you some truths and promises to help you forgive?

_____

_____

"And we know that all things work together for good to those who love God, to those who are the called according to His purpose" (Romans 8:28). What truth and promises can you gather from this verse?

_____

_____

Now write out the three Rs for unforgiveness. For each lie, write a truth. Feel free to use additional paper.

_____

_____

_____

Prayer

Lord, forgiving is hard, but I know I must forgive because You have forgiven me. Help me do this, because I cannot do it on my own. In Jesus's name. Amen.

DAY 45

Toxic People

*Then she called the name of the Lord who spoke to
her, You-Are-the-God-Who-Sees; for she said, "Have
I also here seen Him who sees me?"*

Genesis 16:13

SOMETIMES GOD'S PEOPLE DON'T ACT LIKE GOD'S PEOPLE.
Dysfunctional families occupy most of the first book of the Bible.
We have all experienced church hurt to some degree. We don't expect
Christians to wound us, but I have tasted the bitter heartache of cliqu-
ish people who refuse to allow others in. I've also received hugs given
in love as they stab me in the back.

The patriarch Abram and his wife Sarai mistreated the Egyptian
slave, Hagar. When Sarai hadn't conceived the son of promise, she
told Abram to take Hagar and use her as a surrogate mother without today's modern equipment, if you know what I mean. Once she
became pregnant, the two women grew antagonistic toward one
another. Then Sarai dealt harshly with Hagar, and she left to wander
in the wilderness (Genesis 16:6).

How did Hagar feel when this God-loving couple treated her
like a possession rather than another human being created in the
image of God? That's enough to make you want to give up on God
forever—but God sought Hagar. The Angel of the Lord asked Hagar
where she was going. The *Angel of the Lord* refers to a pre-incarnate
appearance of Jesus Christ.

Does it disturb you that the Angel of the Lord told Hagar to return to this unloving and harsh couple? Perhaps so, if we didn't know the character of our Lord. He would never send a woman back into a potentially abusive situation. God bestowed abundant blessings upon Hagar and her unborn son, Ishmael, and Hagar obediently returned. Sending Hagar back instead of allowing her to roam the wilderness while pregnant seemed like the safest thing for Hagar.

Hagar found comfort in the fact that God saw her and her affliction.

Put distance between yourself and toxic people. When that's impossible, work toward a peaceful atmosphere, whether that includes reconciliation or not. Don't allow them to continue poisoning your heart and mind. Don't allow abuse of any kind to continue. When we get hurt by Christians, it feels like a low blow. We must remember that even though people have been born again, they still live in bodies of flesh, capable of making mistakes.

God sees and He hears. He found Hagar in the wilderness, and He won't leave you in your wilderness either.

Ponder and Practice

Sweet friend, are there any toxic people in your life right now? Have you been wounded by friendly fire in the past? I want to give you this gentle reminder: God sees you, and He sees all your heartache. He has witnessed the rejection and the backstabbing you have endured. Allow God to deal with your pain and those who caused it as He dealt with Sarai and Abram.

We can't control what others do, but we can control our response. How does God want you to handle this situation?

How have you dealt with toxic people in relationships?

_____

_____

_____

How have you dealt with church hurt?

_____

_____

_____

Look up the following verses, and after prayerful consideration, write out a plan concerning how you should handle a toxic relationship: 1 Corinthians 15:33; 2 Timothy 2:16–17; Romans 16:17–18; James 3:16; and Luke 6:27–29.

_____

_____

_____

Prayer

Lord, help me deal with the pain this person has caused me. Help me avoid them when possible. Prevent them from hurting me or others in the future. Help me forgive them. Amen.

DAY 46

Why Is Forgiveness So Hard?

*Jesus said to him, "I do not say to you, up to seven
times, but up to seventy times seven."*

Matthew 18:22

PETER ASKED JESUS HOW MANY TIMES WE HAVE TO FORGIVE. Feeling generous, Peter asked if seven times would be enough. Jesus told Peter we need to forgive seventy times seven, meaning we shouldn't keep a record of wrongs.

My flesh agrees with Peter, but my spirit agrees with Jesus. Do you know someone who names the name of Christ, but continues to hurt you or your family? For years, I dealt with the yo-yo effect. Just when I thought I had forgiven her without any resentment remaining, she committed another offense. Hit rewind and start all over again.

After telling Peter to forgive so many times, Jesus told the parable about the unforgiving servant.

The parable centered on a king who forgave an immense debt owed by one of his servants. Instead of showing the same compassion he'd received, the servant demanded payment from everyone who owed him money. Then the king called the servant out on his unforgiving heart.

Friend, forgiving is hard, but we don't want Jesus calling us out on an unforgiving spirit nor do we want it blocking our blessings and answers to prayer.

I forgive because I am forgiven.

We put ourselves in a prison when we don't forgive, but the key is repentance. We look at the massive sin debt we owed and Christ forgave. Unlike the unforgiving servant, we realize we must forgive those who harm us. Does that mean we will feel all warm and fuzzy? No. Does it mean we have to trust that person again? No. We release them and what they did to Christ, knowing His blood has covered our sins and their sins also.

Understanding why we don't want to forgive might help us forgive. Our flesh wants to hang on to bitterness and anger, but we can't continue walking in the flesh.

We don't want to live in bondage to our flesh any longer. Forgiveness sets us free from that person's hold on us. Let's ask God to help us walk out of the prison of unforgiveness.

Ponder and Practice

Read the parable of the unforgiving servant (Matthew 18:23–35). Notice how much the servant owed the king (Matthew 18:24).

According to John MacArthur, the talent was the largest denomination of currency in that time. Ten thousand represented an infinite number and not necessarily the exact amount the servant owed.[19] How much did our sin debt cost?

For what have you been forgiven by Jesus Christ?

_____

_____

_____

Perhaps you question your salvation. Now would be a great time to get that right. If you have any doubts that you have been forgiven, pray and ask Christ to forgive you. When you do this with a genuinely repentant heart, He will forgive you all your sins—past, present, and future. Tell Him You want to live for Him now and not yourself. If you prayed this prayer and genuinely meant it from the heart, welcome to the family of God.

Who do you need to forgive right now?

_____

_____

Prayer

Lord Jesus, thank You for paying my sin debt. I know I need to forgive this person who has caused so much pain. I can't do it apart from You. I forgive this person because You have forgiven me. Please make this real in my heart. In Jesus's name. Amen.

DAY 47

Can the Relationship Be Restored?

Bearing with one another, and forgiving one another,
if anyone has a complaint against another; even
as Christ forgave you, so you also must do.

Colossians 3:13

THE FORMER PRISONER OF WAR, CORRIE TEN BOOM, STOOD FACING
the vicious guard who had shamed her and the other women as he
glared at them taking their showers. She remembered him, but he
didn't recognize her. Yet here they stood face to face. He extended
his hand seeking forgiveness.

Corrie ten Boom had finished her message on forgiveness when
he approached her. She recognized him as one of her prison guards
from the concentration camp where Corrie and her sister Betsy had
been sent. He explained how God had forgiven him, but now he asked
her to forgive him too. Corrie explained how she wrestled with unforgiveness in that moment. Then she took his hand and said the words,
"I forgive you." She also explained how amazing it felt to forgive out
of obedience to the Lord.[20]

I haven't needed to forgive someone for something so heinous,
and I hope I never will. I'd like to think I could do the right thing.
How can we forgive so much, and how can relationships be restored
after trust has been broken?

That person doesn't deserve our forgiveness, but we didn't deserve
Christ's forgiveness either.

Paul encouraged his readers in Colossae to forgive those who wronged them, and through this letter he penned centuries ago, he encourages us to do likewise. What if the person needing our forgiveness is a spouse or close family member? Can we forgive unfaithfulness? Can we forgive heartache? Can we forgive intentional affliction?

Forgiveness is the first step down a long road. If you want to seek reconciliation, the next step will be restoration. We cannot control people's actions, nor can we fix them, but God can.

Can we meet that extended hand and forgive like Corrie ten Boom? Forgiveness doesn't include moving toward restoration unless trust can be rebuilt. Only time will reveal if the relationship can be restored. Without that bond of trust, reconciliation cannot occur. God only commands we forgive. We decide whether or not to continue in the relationship.

Friend, if you find yourself standing at the crossroads of forgiveness and restoration, I would love to pray for you. Even now, as I type, I pray for you. Ask God to direct your heart.

Ponder and Practice

Broken hearts and broken relationships demand God's armor. Read Psalm 147:3. Rewrite this verse as your belt of truth. Add any additional verses that will help you focus on God's truth and not the enemy's lies.

_____

_____

What verse can be your breastplate of righteousness?

_____

_____

Choose a verse to act as your shoes of peace (John 16:33; Colossians 3:15; or Philippians 4:8 are possibilities).

_____

_____

The helmet of salvation protects our minds. Which memories and thoughts are toxic?

_____

_____

Using the shield of faith, what will you trust God to do in this relationship?

_____

_____

Remember the sword of the Spirit is your only offensive weapon. What is it?

_____

_____

Prayer

Lord, help me forgive this person. Show me Your will. Should we work toward reconciliation? Help the memories stop attacking me, reopening old wounds. Heal my heart and heal this relationship if this is Your will. In Jesus's name. Amen.

DAY 48

The Nakedness of Shame

So he said, "I heard Your voice in the garden, and I was afraid because I was naked; and I hid myself."

Genesis 3:10

I SPENT MOST OF MY LIFE FEELING ASHAMED OF MY DISABILITY, BUT now I consider this visual impairment as a gift from God. Bullying and rejection from my peers during childhood left me scarred. It followed me into adulthood, but God has helped me overcome it in recent years.

The first negative emotion to make its grand entrance into the world was shame, and fear followed. Both occurred as a result of sin.

Moments after Adam and Eve ate the forbidden fruit, God opened their eyes. They became aware of their nakedness, and shame enveloped them. Then they heard God in the garden of Eden, and fear took them hostage as they tried to hide from God.

Not much has changed since Eden. Shame continues to leave us exposed, and many people still try to hide from God. Many still try to cover up their humiliation.

Once God found the first couple, He dealt with their sin. Then He did the same thing He wants to do for us. God covered what shame uncovered.

God killed two animals, and He made tunics for Adam and Eve with the animal skins. The bloodshed symbolized the blood of Christ, shed on the cross to cover our sin and our shame. The fig leaves Adam and Eve had used to try to hide their shame didn't involve a blood sacrifice. God gave them the skins of dead animals to remind them of the bloodshed.

Are you carrying the burden of yesterday's guilt—maybe even today's guilt? Jesus shed His blood to atone for our sins. He welcomes a contrite heart, and He stands ready to forgive a repentant sinner.

Perhaps the enemy continues to remind you of a life you regret. If you have been born again, that sin has been covered along with its accompanying guilt. Refuse to allow the devil to taunt you with painful reminders.

Maybe your sin doesn't haunt you but the sin of another. It leaves you feeling naked and incomplete, like a victim. Love covers what shame uncovered.

God is love, and His love covers the nakedness of shame, just like the tunics He made for Adam and Eve. He wants you to take His hand and leave the victim mentality behind because He has made you a victor.

Ponder and Practice

With much practice the enemy has skillfully mastered the tactic of shame. Each time the memory of that horrible event rushes to the forefront of your mind, forbid it to stay. Allow God's love to reign in both your heart and your mind.

Write down each shameful incident that haunts you. Use a bold marker to write *forgiven* over each one. As you complete this activity, pray about each circumstance as you forever release it to God.

_____

_____

_____

_____

_____

Write out your three Rs for the shame and guilt you feel. If necessary, use an additional sheet of paper, because you must address each one.

_____

_____

_____

What lies has God revealed?

Remove the lies and replace them with God's truth.

Shame cannot expose what God has covered. Ask God to conquer those memories and feelings so you can live forgiven.

Prayer

Heavenly Father, rescue me from the continual guilt I feel over forgiven sin and shame. Remove the memories of sinful, horrific acts of others. Remove the memory as far as the east is from the west, which is what You do with our sin. Heal me from the pain and shame. In Jesus's name. Amen.

DAY 49

Shame's Misery

*And she was in bitterness of soul, and prayed
to the Lord and wept in anguish.*

1 Samuel 1:10

WHEN I READ ABOUT HANNAH, I SEE JESUS. THEN I SEE MY SIN. MY flesh wants to slap Hannah's husband and his second wife, who bullied Hannah. But not Hannah; Hannah fulfilled the meaning of her name—gracious.

Have you ever asked *why me?* Hannah felt the emptiness of her womb, bearing the great shame of infertility that existed in biblical times. Misery enveloped her as she wept so much that she had no appetite. The constant badgering from her husband's other wife, Peninnah, who had children, added to the weight of Hannah's burden. Shame and misery meet at the intersection of sin.

We find misery woven throughout Scripture from Adam and Eve after the fall in Genesis to the letter to the Laodiceans in Revelation. Jesus said, "I counsel you to buy from Me gold refined in the fire, that you may be rich; and white garments, that you may be clothed, *that the shame of your nakedness may not be revealed*" (Revelation 3:18).

In both the Genesis and Revelation accounts, we see a connection between nakedness and shame. God clothed Adam and Eve, and He offered white garments to the Laodiceans.

What heinous sin created misery and shame for Hannah? Sometimes, we bear shame from the sin of others. Consider a woman who has been raped or sexually abused. Her misery is born out of someone else's sin, not her own.

I wore shame for most of my life for being different. Hannah's shame came from society's belittling attitude about infertile women.

What changed for Hannah? What changed for me? What will change your life?

Hannah prayed for a son, promising she would return him to the Lord. She went in her affliction and sorrow to the only source of mercy, God. Hannah's name also means mercy.

God exchanges our rags of misery for His riches of mercy.

He stands ready to cover our shame with garments of righteousness. He cleanses the guilt of repentant sinners. He washes away the victim mentality from someone carrying shame. God makes victors out of victims. He gives children to the childless, and he dresses us in clothes of mercy.

Has your sin, or perhaps someone else's sin, caused you shame? When we take our junk to God—everything from misery to shame— He showers us with His merciful riches. Let's enter the throne room of grace.

Ponder and Practice

How can we use the armor of God to combat shame? Discover your own Scriptures or use the options given to design a battle strategy against shame and the misery that accompanies it. Here are some options, but by now, you probably know the best verses for yourself: Matthew 5:7; Isaiah 43:18–19; Psalm 103:8; or Hebrews 2:11.

What is your belt of truth?

_____

_____

Your breastplate of righteousness?

_____

_____

Shoes of peace?

_____

_____

Helmet of salvation?

_____

_____

Shield of faith?

_____

_____

Sword of the Spirit?

_____

_____

Prayer

Lord, please remove my burden of shame and misery. I know I shouldn't carry it any longer. Clothe me in Your mercy. Amen.

DAY 50

Shame from the Religious Crowd

Then He said to the woman, "Your faith has saved you. Go in peace."
Luke 7:50

YOU OVERHEAR ALMOST EVERYTHING IN A SMALL CHURCH, INCLUD-
ing the name of the visitor sitting in the back. I recognized the name
from my past. Most Sundays I could stare straight ahead and refrain
from looking around, but not today. Within minutes, I had to stand
up and speak, facing my past. Soon peace replaced my nervousness
because God reminded me I had no reason to feel ashamed. He had
transformed my messed-up life into a masterpiece.

Simon, a Pharisee, invited Jesus to dinner. Tradition allowed
spectators to attend such dinners, but the appearance of a well-known
prostitute would have shocked everyone there—except Jesus.

The passage in Luke chapter 7 leads us to believe she had repented
and turned to Christ in recent hours or days. Now she came to worship
her Savior. She wept over His feet, allowing her hair to fall down,
something then considered disgraceful. She wiped Jesus's feet with her
hair. She broke an expensive bottle of perfume and anointed His feet.

She couldn't hear the condemning thoughts rolling around in
Simon's head, but Jesus knew the self-righteous thoughts. In response,
Jesus told Simon a parable, explaining that one who has been forgiven
much will love much. Then Jesus compared the actions of this scan-
dalous woman to those of Simon.

Simon had welcomed Jesus with neither a kiss nor water to clean His feet as was customary in that day.

This unnamed woman had done all that. Now Jesus spoke to the woman. "Your faith has saved you. Go in peace" (Luke 7:50).

Whispers spread around the table. *How can He forgive sins?*

We all have a past. Jesus wants to cover our faith in the same peace He gave that woman long ago. We possess that peace because our faith has saved us, and we are at peace with God.

Simon couldn't grasp the fact that this lowliest of women had a place in the kingdom of God. He saw her sin, but he couldn't see his own sin. He might have held a high position in society, but unless something changed, he had no place in God's kingdom.

Friend, if you have received Jesus's free gift of salvation, don't allow anyone to look down their pharisaical nose at you. Possess the courage of this forgiven prostitute and hold your head high. People will see the transforming work of God in your life.

Ponder and Practice

Read the passage in Luke 7:35–50. Keep in mind that Jesus knew Simon's thoughts, and Simon never said anything derogatory about the woman out loud.

What types of nonverbal language could Simon have used that would have conveyed his feelings toward this sinful woman?

_____

_____

_____

When have you experienced either verbal or nonverbal slurs?

_____

_____

_____

How do you think this woman felt?

How do you think she felt when Jesus spoke so highly of her?

_____

_____

_____

Would your church welcome someone into your congregation even if they needed a bath? A homeless person? An alcoholic?

_____

_____

How does the condescension of self-righteous people affect people like this woman?

_____

_____

_____

What might their actions lead them to believe?

_____

_____

_____

Write out the three Rs for yourself, a friend, or this woman in Luke.

_____

_____

_____

Prayer

Heavenly Father, thank You for loving me no matter what I have done or who I was before I met You. Help me never look down on others because they haven't come to know You like I have. In Jesus's name. Amen.

PART VI

Discouragement, Depression, and Grief

DAY 51

God, Where Are You?

For You are the God of my strength; Why do You cast me off?
Why do I go mourning because of the oppression of the enemy?

Psalm 43:2

I'VE ASKED THAT SAME QUESTION. GOD GREETS ME IN PRAYER, BUT not last night, this morning, or this afternoon. A spiritual wall blocked me from His presence when I needed Him to rescue me from the incredible pain I suffered. Not a physical pain, but an emotional one so intense that I considered suicide to flee from its long-reaching tentacles.

I found myself fighting depression alone. Had I known our focal verse echoed my trauma, I might have turned there and prayed through the entire psalm.

What a relief to know the psalmist felt that same emptiness. He cried out for the God of his strength.

I didn't recognize the spiritual battle raging within me. The enemy hissed lies in my head. *He's abandoned you.* I held onto Hebrews 13:5 like a life jacket that kept me afloat until the healing came, for He Himself has said, "I will never leave you nor forsake you" (Hebrews 13:5).

I stopped asking, "Where are You, God?" I began declaring, "You haven't left me." The psalmist mourned from the oppression of the enemy, like me and perhaps like you. Look at how the psalmist prays: "Oh, send out Your light and Your truth" (Psalm 43:3).

Jesus Christ is the light of the world (John 8:12). He is the way, the truth, and the life (John 14:6). Compare Jesus to the darkness of the enemy and his lies. That's all he speaks—lies.

The light of Jesus never dims. Nor does it ever go out.

Unlike the psalmist, we don't have to find a church, tabernacle, or altar to pray. We can meet with God anytime and anywhere.

Friend, if you can't shake discouragement or depression, I beg you to do two things. See a doctor, because antidepressants do help. Second, stop believing your feelings of abandonment. He hasn't left you, and He will never forsake you. You can make it, like the psalmist and myself.

The enemy loves playing mind games, taking advantage of our despair or a medical chemical imbalance. We don't recognize his tricks as easily when dark clouds of suffering surround us. Friend, we must draw on God's strength in our weakest moments, especially when we cannot detect His presence. He is still there.

Ponder and Practice

I didn't know then what I know now about spiritual warfare and dressing in the armor of God. The wealth of information I am sharing with you now came through trials and in-depth study in the Word of God. How I wish someone had come along and shown me how to dress in the believer's armor. Since we're coming to the end of our journey together, I encourage you to seek out the Bible verses you can pray and declare over yourself as you put on the armor one piece at a time. If you get stuck, the psalms provide a wealth of helpful passages, especially Psalms 42 and 43.

Write out Scriptures for the following pieces of armor:

Belt of truth:

_____

_____

Breastplate of righteousness:

_____

_____

Shoes of peace:

_____

_____

Helmet of salvation:

_____

_____

Shield of faith:

_____

_____

Sword of the Spirit:

_____

_____

Prayer

Lord, You agonized about sin-bearing in the garden of Gethsemane. You know the extent of my heartache. Dress me in Your armor. You go before me. You fight my battles. I trust You even while You are silent. Relieve me from this pain. In Jesus's name. Amen.

DAY 52

Finding Joy amid Sorrow

*Then he said to them, "Go your way, eat the fat, drink
the sweet, and send portions to those for whom nothing is prepared; for this day is holy to our Lord. Do not
sorrow, for the joy of the Lord is your strength."*

Nehemiah 8:10

THE EMPTY CHAIR AT THE TABLE MAKES HOLIDAY CELEBRATIONS
difficult. A deafening silence surrounds us at each meal. My greatest
sorrow came when my daughter became the prodigal. How would I
survive? Would I ever taste joy again?

The exiled Jews returned from Babylon to the ruins of Jerusalem.
Ezra the scribe assembled them in a public square at the Water Gate
as he read from the Book of the Law. The Water Gate represents
the ministry of God's Word. When they heard the Scriptures, they
mourned over their sin.

Nehemiah told the Jews, "Go your way, eat the fat, drink the
sweet." He knew grief can immobilize people, locking them in a place
they cannot escape. The first nugget we gleam from Nehemiah tells us
to move forward. God doesn't expect us to move in leaps and bounds
but to make baby steps so we don't become stagnant.

God cares about our physical needs when we mourn. He knows
we need nourishment, so Nehemiah told the people to enjoy their food
and drink. This stirs up childhood memories when the neighbors

stocked our kitchen with casseroles and cakes whenever a family member passed on.

Next, feed your joy by giving to others. At the right time, seek to share with someone who has a need. Giving super infuses our joy.

Then Nehemiah declared, "The joy of the Lord is your strength." During a sermon from December 2021, my pastor, Adam Williams, stated that the literal translation is "The light of Jehovah is a strong refuge." God, our only source of true joy, shelters us while we sorrow. His joy fuels us on as we move forward.

Joy doesn't abandon us during grief. Joy surrounds us in the comfort of God and His Word. We find it in the faces of friends and family.

The world can experience only happiness. The world has never tasted pure joy. When we open our Bibles and allow God's Word to comfort our sorrowful hearts, we will sense the abiding joy deep within.

Ponder and Practice
Read John 16:20. According to this verse, what happens with our sorrow?

_____

_____

_____

List the three things Nehemiah, through the inspiration of the Holy Spirit, directed the Jews and us to do when we grieve (Nehemiah 8:10).

_____

_____

_____

Nehemiah told the people not to grieve over their sin any longer. Although the grief of the Jews is much different from grief over losing someone we love, we can still find help in this passage.

Notice I didn't suggest we stop grieving, as Nehemiah did. Why did Nehemiah tell them to stop grieving over their sin?

_____

_____

_____

What has God shown you from today's passage?

_____

_____

_____

God created us with the ability to cry when we grieve. Grief varies from the other emotions we have discussed since it's a natural part of life. When would grief become an emotional stronghold?

_____

_____

_____

Have you ever faced grief as an unnatural stronghold? How could someone break free from that?

_____

_____

_____

Prayer

> *Lord God*, thank You for Your loving care for us. You help us in our grief. You care about our spiritual and physical nourishment. Help me through these days of mourning, and help me move forward, fueled by Your joy. In Jesus's name. Amen.

DAY 53

Our Great Heart Surgeon

He heals the brokenhearted and binds up their wounds.
Psalm 147:3

WHEN TIMMY LOST HIS BROTHER TO LIVER DISEASE, HE SUFFERED from broken heart syndrome, or stress cardiomyopathy, and it almost killed him. Timmy woke me up. "I can't breathe!"

I dialed 911. Placing my hands on Timmy's back, I prayed. While we waited for the rescue squad, he began coughing and spitting stuff up. I didn't recognize the symptoms as congestive heart failure even though my mom had it years earlier.

At the hospital, a breathing treatment allowed him to breathe easier. The doctor diagnosed him with a flash form of heart failure. The next day, another doctor discussed Timmy's circumstances with him. After learning about Timmy's brother's recent death, she told us that broken heart syndrome can occur when you don't grieve properly.

Timmy's focus following his brother's death centered around his mother, but they grieved in opposite ways. She wanted every memory of her son removed from the house, but Timmy wasn't ready to go through his brother's belongings. He didn't take time to grieve.

Friend, if you have lost someone you love, take time to grieve. Grieving is healing, and God is our great heart surgeon.

Let's revisit the ruins of Jerusalem when Nehemiah encouraged the brokenhearted Jews. An unknown author penned Psalm 147 after

233

they restored their beloved city.[21] The verbs *heals* and *binds* connote a continual healing and binding, one with no end.

Are you heartbroken today? Are you wounded with sorrows? Focus on Christ rather than the immediate crisis. Do you see Him healing and binding up your wounds? We cannot escape seasons of grief, but God never intended for us to navigate our mourning alone.

Take the time you need to tend to your wounds before they progress into a physical health problem. Never forget your Comforter holds your hand.

We mourn because we've loved someone worth mourning over. You have precious memories of your loved one. Right now, they create pain, but thank God for these memories and the unique gift God gave you by placing your loved one in your life.

Look for God's comfort today because He has an intimate knowledge of your pain. It might appear in a hug, the song of a bird, the beauty of a flower, or a Bible verse. Let Him hold you while you cry.

Ponder and Practice
Read 2 Corinthians 1:3–7. The word *comfort* in this passage connotes helping and making one stronger. With that in mind, what does this passage say to you?

_____

_____

_____

What does this passage tell us about God?

_____

_____

_____

When does God comfort us (verse 4)?

_____

_____

_____

What does verse 5 say about suffering and consolation?

_____

_____

_____

Why does God comfort us (verse 4)?

_____

_____

_____

Who can you share some comfort with today?

_____

_____

_____

In verse 6, the word _enduring_ reflects the idea of a triumphant spirit. With that in mind, what is God saying to you through this verse? Take time to pray, asking the Holy Spirit to clarify this for you.

_____

_____

_____

What is one action step you can take away from today's devotion and reflection? When and how will you implement this?

_____

_____

_____

Prayer

Heavenly Father and God of all comfort, thank You for Your continual healing of my heart. Today I need Your comfort as I mourn. I also ask You to comfort my loved one who is grieving today. Help us grieve well, and help us comfort others. In Jesus's name. Amen.

DAY 54

From Drought to Drowning

*Why are you cast down, O my soul? And why are you
disquieted within me? Hope in God, for I shall yet
praise Him for the help of His countenance.*

Psalm 42:5

WOULD A DAY COME WHEN I DIDN'T CRY ANYMORE? I HAD LOST MY
entire family, except for my husband. My mother lived in a locked
down Alzheimer's unit, and my daughter had broken all ties with us.
I missed her in a house filled with silence.

The doctor diagnosed me with clinical depression. The antidepressants helped, but I wanted to break free from the medication.
Antidepressants carry a stigma in the church. This tragedy prevents
many people from getting the help they need.

Psalm 42 begins with a thirst for God, like a man lost in an arid
land without water. The psalmist longed to visit the temple, where the
presence of God dwelled. In his depression, he heard the whispering
of the enemy: *God doesn't care about you, or He would rescue you
from this turmoil.*

The psalmist asks the same questions we do: *Why am I depressed?
Has God abandoned me? As a Christian, I shouldn't be trapped in a
prison of darkness, should I?*

The word translated *disquieted* in our focal verse means uneasy or
lacking peace.[22] The NIV translates it as *disturbed*, and the Christian
Standard Bible (CSB) uses *in turmoil*. Have you ever felt like that?

Then the psalmist reminded himself that hope exists in Elohim, the creator God who created something out of nothing. Hope arises out of the ashes as he believed God would deliver him from such agony.

Then like the ebb and flow of the tide, the darkness returned, but this time he compared it to drowning. If you have battled depression or anxiety, you might recognize the roller-coaster ride of emotions.

The psalmist concluded with the same promise of hope and praise. When I read Psalms 42 and 43, I connect with the author. He experienced everything I did. He reminds me of hope in the dark, like a candle in a dark room. Darkness must flee.

Hope's light never dims, nor does it ever go out.

Never forget the importance of praise that accompanies hope. When the tears flow, praise God. The devil can't stand watching us worship in our darkest hour. Give him heartburn and bring heaven down to earth.

Ponder and Practice
Read Psalm 42. Many commentators believe David wrote this psalm, but others believe the sons of Korah wrote it. Whatever the name of the author, this psalm reflects the deep despair of a child of God. When have you sought God with the same urgency expressed in verse 1?

_____

_____

_____

The Old Testament saints had to travel to the temple to meet with God. We are blessed beyond measure because we can come boldly to the throne room of grace. When have you experienced a time when you felt abandoned by God?

_____

_____

_____

Read Matthew 5:3–4. How do you think God feels about depression?

_____

_____

_____

Write out the three Rs for yourself, the psalmist, or someone drowning in the sea of depression.

_____

_____

_____

Prayer

Heavenly Father, thank You for not condemning me for battling the chemical imbalance known as depression. You don't condescend when I feel anxious. You love and comfort me. You give me hope, and You always deliver me. I praise You because You resurrect dead things and You are a good Father. In Jesus's name. Amen.

DAY 55

When a Sheep Needs Its Shepherd

He restores my soul.
Psalm 23:3

MY WILLPOWER TO GET OUT OF BED OR EAT DISAPPEARED LIKE THE sun behind a black cloud. I drenched my pillow with tears. One of my darkest days with depression occurred after learning my prodigal daughter wanted no reunion. She wouldn't even pick up the phone to call me. She preferred a life free from rules and God.

A sheep that has lain down, stretched out in the sun, and rolled into a comfortable position on his back is called a cast sheep. When the sheep tries to stand up, his feet can't make contact with the ground. Struggling only tires the sheep. Unless the shepherd intervenes, he will die. Either the heat of the day or a watchful predator will end the sheep's life.[23]

Weight works against the sheep's ability to get back on its feet. Whether heavy with wool, fat, or pregnancy, the weight works against the sheep.

Friend, sometimes we carry a weight we cannot bear. Discouragement, disappointment, depression, or grief makes getting through the day a struggle. Like a cast sheep, we need our Good Shepherd to set us upright again.

As David penned the twenty-third Psalm, he might have recalled the multiple times he had rescued a cast sheep. Then his thoughts drifted to the countless times God had delivered him.

Jesus turns our upside-down world right side up again.

As I traveled through depression, my husband feared he'd come home to discover I had given in to suicidal thoughts. That particular day, he found me in bed. He demanded, "Get out of bed and get dressed! We're going out to dinner."

"I'm not hungry."

"I am, so get up and get dressed."

Having no other choice, I dressed and got in the car, and I made it through dinner without falling apart. In retrospect, Timmy gave me exactly what I needed to make it through that day.

In time and with medication, the depression subsided. Joy returned, but if Jesus hadn't restored my soul, I would have been another cast-sheep casualty.

Friend, are you that cast sheep today? No matter what you try, you can't find relief? Cry out to Jesus. Let Him hear your continual bleating. Jesus, our Good Shepherd, restores our souls.

Ponder and Practice

Wool can be symbolic of the world and the old life before Christ.[24] The Levitical priests couldn't wear wool in the Holy of Holies (Leviticus 16:4).

As you've discovered through our study about negative emotions, the flesh can become controlling at times. Fear, worry, stress, and a multitude of undesired emotions can imprison us. The flesh wallows in discouragement and disappointment, magnifying the problem; we cannot cope when depression or grief consumes us.

When the sheep get heavy with wool, the shepherd shears them. When we become entangled in the world or recognize emotional strongholds, we need shearing from the world, the flesh, and the devil. When have you needed shearing?

Can you create a plan using the three R's to combat those situations?

_____

_____

_____

Prayer

> *Lord Jesus,* I don't recognize my world anymore. Hear my cries and restore my soul! Restore the joy and peace I have lost in my hopeless state. Thank You, Lord, for the day when weeping will turn into joy. In Jesus's name. Amen.

DAY 56

Why Do We Have to Travel through the Valley?

Yea, though I walk through the valley of the
shadow of death, I will fear no evil;
For You are with me; Your rod and Your staff, they comfort me.

Psalm 23:4

I EXPERIENCED THE WORST YEAR OF MY LIFE IN 2006. I KEPT MY MOM in her home as long as possible, but as her dementia worsened, she required a skilled nursing facility. Dementia robs the patient of their memory, beginning with short-term memories until they forget how to feed themselves. It robs the family of their loved one long before they leave this world. The valley of 2006 also included a wayward daughter, and I slipped into a deep depression.

Each year, the shepherd leads his flock through the dark valley, the only route to higher ground. Christians might not travel through valleys annually. Sometimes, we make that treacherous journey more often.

The only way to reach the mountaintop is through the valley.

Before leading his flock to the mountaintop, the shepherd makes the trip alone. He removes potential dangers such as poisonous plants, but he can't eliminate everything. Rockslides, floods, and clever predators lurk among the cliffs.

We desire to speed up our dark route, but notice we *walk* through the valley. We don't *run* through it. During our hike, we will receive some blessings amid the despair.

A valley provides refreshing water for the sheep. Our Good Shepherd, Jesus, offers us that same refreshment as we drink in the living water. Valleys also make great grazing ground for the flock. While we travel through the valleys of life, we maintain our strength by grazing upon the Word of God.

Three years later, my mom passed through the valley of the shadow of death—a *shadow*, not an end. She took her last breath on earth, but she took her next one in heaven. Perfect memory. Perfect knowledge.

Relief washed over me since I no longer had to watch her suffer. My grief began years earlier when she slipped away from the vital woman she once was. My shepherd walked through that valley with both of us. It ended as my mom and I reached two different mountaintops.

Are you on that journey today? Drink in the refreshment that comes only from the painful crevices of life. Allow the Word to nourish you, and know your Good Shepherd walks beside you each step of the way.

Ponder and Practice

The shepherd used his rod to protect his flock from predators. What modern-day predators do we face?

_____

_____

_____

The shepherd uses his staff to guide the sheep, much like the Holy Spirit directs us. How have you seen the Holy Spirit directing you through a valley?

_____

_____

_____

What blessings have you found in the dark valleys?

_____

_____

Describe at least one mountaintop experience that occurred after your journey through the valley.

_____

_____

_____

What did God protect you from in those valleys?

_____

_____

_____

"Blessed are those who mourn, for they shall be comforted" (Matthew 5:4). How has God comforted you in your times of mourning?

_____

_____

_____

As you travel through the valley, how can you concentrate more on the refreshment of Jesus and the nourishment of Scripture?

_____

_____

_____

God controls the valley. How does that give you peace and assurance?

_____

_____

_____

Prayer

Lord Jesus, You are my living water as I travel paths I'd rather not navigate. Refresh me as I graze upon Your Word. Thank You for walking with me and for the mountaintop we will reach. In Jesus's name. Amen.

DAY 57

It's Okay to Ask Why

And about the ninth hour Jesus cried out with a loud voice, saying, "Eli, Eli, lama sabachthani?" that is, "My God, My God, why have You forsaken Me?"

Matthew 27:46

MY FRIEND SAT STILL, HEAD BOWED AS TEARS SLIPPED DOWN HER cheeks. She dabbed them with a tissue, but they refused to subside. "Why, God?" She had been a pastor's wife with a special needs grandchild, and now she missed her late husband with a deep sorrow.

Guilt consumed her for questioning God, until a friend showed her that even Jesus asked why.

Jesus, the God-Man, didn't need to ask that question. He knew all things, but in His agonizing death on the cross, He did ask.

But what about never question God? Two types of people ask why. One doubts God. They question His judgments and plans. They wonder if God knows what He is doing. The second type of person who asks why has a genuine desire for answers. This motive for asking reveals a desire to know God and a humility that realizes how finite our understanding is.

Why does my child have special needs? Why did God take my husband so soon? Why did God allow that horrific accident? Why does my child have cancer?

Warren W. Wiersbe says, "This was not the cry of a complaining servant, but the sob of a brokenhearted child. Asking where is my Father when I need him."[25]

Asking why isn't sinful. We must examine our motive for asking. Do we search for answers to questions, or do we ask in doubt? Asking in faith characterizes a heart seeking the will of God and not their own self-will. We seek to know the mind of Christ when we ask why (1 Corinthians 2:16).

Asking why isn't sinful when a sincere heart seeks answers.

Do you live with guilt because, like most of us, you have asked why? Break free from that guilt today. Never go there again, because even Jesus asked His Father why. Saints from across the ages have done the same thing: David, Asaph, and Moses. Celebrate your victory because you can ask why.

Ponder and Practice

"If any of you lacks wisdom, let him ask of God, who gives to all liberally and without reproach, and it will be given to him. But let him ask in faith, with no doubting, for he who doubts is like a wave of the sea driven and tossed by the wind" (James 1:5–6).

James, under the inspiration of the Holy Spirit, encourages us to seek wisdom. In what situations would you seek God's wisdom?

_____

_____

_____

How does God distribute wisdom according to this passage?

_____

_____

James goes on to call the one doubting a "double-minded man" (James 1:8). Why is that description appropriate?

_____

_____

_____

Why does James compare the doubtful man to a wave of the sea tossed by the wind?

_____

_____

_____

If you have asked God why, what was your motive?

_____

_____

_____

Write out your three Rs for seeking answers from God.

_____

_____

_____

Prayer

Heavenly Father, I long to understand why bad things happen. Thank You for freeing me from the guilt and shame for seeking Your wisdom. I trust You, but understanding some things baffles me. In Jesus's name. Amen.

DAY 58

What Are We Doing Here?

And there he went into a cave, and spent the night in that place; and behold, the word of the Lord came to him, and He said to him, "What are you doing here, Elijah?"

1 Kings 19:9

I EMBRACED MY INDEPENDENCE AS I STEPPED INTO THE ROLE OF Super Blind Woman, not a role designed by God. While Timmy sat at his dying brother's bedside in North Carolina, I thought I could do everything: buy groceries, feed his brother's dog next door, and order my toothpaste online. We hadn't prepared for this situation, and I had never done any of this before. We had been thrown into an impossible situation.

Frustration loomed over me as I swiped through multiple varieties of toothpaste on my phone. *Which one do I use?* Since that didn't work out, I decided to feed the dog. Off I went, across our driveway with my white cane. When I returned home, the driveway and street felt the same. I found myself lost right in front of my house. Somehow, I made it to my back door, disappointed in myself and God. Never mind that He got me safely home.

Pressure intensified with a publishing pitfall, and I slipped into the downward spiral of depression. A combination of failed expectations and self-reliance brought on the pity party.

Elijah had experienced his Mount Carmel victory against the prophets of Baal, but he soon took a downward spiral when wicked

Queen Jezebel sent him a warning. She threatened to kill Elijah. Now fear captured this bold prophet, who had once taken a stand for God. He ran scared.

Alone and far from Jezebel, Elijah asked God to take his life (1 Kings 19:4). Things didn't turn out the way he expected.

God asked Elijah, "What are you doing here?" God asked me the same question as I felt incapable of doing anything, and I, too, begged God to take my life.

We can fall into discouragement or even depression when life takes a quick detour. God doesn't meet our expectations, and we develop a me-first attitude.

An inward focus sets us up for a downfall.

God's question took Elijah's thoughts off the poor-me exit ramp and put him onto "Focus on God Highway." Friend, do failed expectations exacerbate your despair? God is asking you the same question: What are you doing here?

Ponder and Practice

Surely you have felt disappointment, despair, or depression at some point because your expectations weren't met like you thought they should be.

In what ways would you consider your current expectations realistic or unrealistic?

_____

_____

_____

In the midst of depression, our thoughts turn inward. After hearing from other women about their experiences with depression, I realized how self-focused we become, but we cannot see that while we are in the thick of depression. When have you experienced times of self-centered thoughts?

_____

_____

_____

God wants us to depend solely on Him. Sometimes, He has to peel back our self-reliance and show us just how much we need Him. I left God out when I put on my superhero cape, but I discovered I couldn't order my own toothpaste, much less conquer my neighborhood. When have you relied on self and not God?

_____

_____

_____

How did it turn out?

_____

_____

_____

Prayer

Lord, I can do nothing apart from You. Thank You for always helping me, even when I shut You out. Help me not focus on faulty expectations but trust in You for everything. Amen.

DAY 59

God Won't Leave You There

So he arose, and ate and drank; and he went in the strength of that
food forty days and forty nights as far as Horeb, the mountain of God.

1 Kings 19:8

MY SPEAKING MINISTRY SHUT DOWN WITH THE ARRIVAL OF COVID.
Defeat imprisoned me, and I didn't try to escape—until God freed me.

You don't have to struggle with grief or depression to get stuck in
the quicksand of despair and disappointment, but I have good news!
God won't leave you there.

Let's revisit this account in 1 Kings 19. In Elijah's depression,
God sent an angel to attend to his physical needs with food and water.
Our focal verse displays the power of God's refreshment. Elijah traveled through the wilderness for forty days until he came to Horeb,
also known as Mount Sinai, the place where Moses met with God.

After Elijah's pity party, God instructed Elijah to go out and
stand on the mountain. Elijah witnessed howling wind, an earthquake, and fire, but Elijah didn't see God in any of these.

Afterward, God manifested Himself in a still small voice. God
asked the same question. "What are you doing here, Elijah?" (1 Kings
19:13). Elijah still gave his victim-mentality answer. *I'm the only one left*
serving You (1 Kings 19:14).

Then God told Elijah He had seven thousand men in Israel who hadn't turned to Baal worship. Elijah felt all alone, but God revealed the truth, and He commissioned Elijah to anoint his successor, Elisha.

Discouragement, grief, and depression can affect even the most spiritual of people, like Elijah. Those feelings tend to shut us away from God, but we see how God drew Elijah into His presence. He even gave him the strength to get there. Once God had Elijah where He wanted him, God dealt with Elijah's despair.

I wanted to live in victory, but it seemed unobtainable. One Sunday morning, as the praise team sang "See a Victory," God drew me to the altar and into His arms.

Discouragement hides God from us, but we are never hidden from God.

Does discouragement hold you hostage today? Walk into the arms of your heavenly Father, but if you don't, He will draw you in.

God will never leave us in the valley of discouragement. Isn't it wonderful that God gives us time and space, but He always leads us out of the valley?

Ponder and Practice

Describe a season when God met you and led you out of the valley.

_____

_____

_____

What might have happened if Elijah hadn't stepped out of the cave?

_____

_____

_____

Read 1 Kings 19:11–12. Sometimes, we look for God in mighty displays of the supernatural. Up to this time, Elijah had grown accustomed to the supernatural. How does God usually reveal Himself to you?

_____

_____

_____

When I feel discouraged or even depressed, the noise in my head, my own excuses, block out the still small voice of God. What noise or distractions prevent you from hearing God's still small voice?

_____

_____

Read 1 Kings 19:13–14. Most commentators describe Elijah's actions in verse 13 as worship. Use a study Bible or free online resource, such as Bible Gateway or Blue Letter Bible to see what you can find about this verse.

What were Elijah's excuses in verse 14?

_____

_____

We may be victims, but we don't have to possess a victim mentality. What excuses do you offer God that display a victim mentality?

_____

_____

_____

Prayer

Lord God, I'm blessed because You never leave me in the valley. Thank You for drawing me out and into the place of Your healing and restoration. Amen.

DAY 60

A Message from Peter

His divine power has given to us all things that pertain to life and godliness, through the knowledge of Him who called us by glory and virtue.

2 Peter 1:3

I NEVER THOUGHT I'D USE ANYTHING I LEARNED IN MY BIBLIOLOGY course, but here goes. Each word Peter wrote came directly from the Holy Spirit while allowing for Peter's personality. What do Peter and the Holy Spirit want us to know?

We need to know God in an intimate, experiential way. According to Warren W. Wiersbe, Peter uses some form of the word *know* thirteen times in this epistle. Wiersbe describes this knowledge as a "living participation in the truth."[26]

That includes Peter's walk on the Sea of Galilee. The disciples in the boat didn't seek that experience, only Peter. Keep that in mind as we unpack this treasure.

Jesus has given us all things pertaining to life and godliness through His divine power. We must spend time with the Lord to possess such knowledge.

Verse 4 makes the pot sweeter by adding "exceedingly great and precious promises." What a bountiful gift! Why do we live in lack if we have everything Peter describes? We don't appropriate these gifts, such as the armor of God. We feel like paupers, so our feelings boss us around. We don't know what we possess because we don't read our Bibles. We don't spend quality time with Jesus.

Peter called us "partakers of the divine nature" through His promises (2 Peter 1:4). Yet if we don't know His promises, we don't grow.

Warren W. Wiersbe compares these gifts to seeds that needed to receive nourishment.[27] Dr. Tony Evans compares them to a newborn.[28] We must nurture these gifts to full maturity, just like a seedling or baby.

Peter concluded by saying we have escaped "the corruption that is in the world through lust" (2 Peter 1:4). My friend, how can we live like redeemed children of God and not the unbelievers of the world? We start good habits, but then we get sidetracked. When we fail to abide in Christ, take thoughts captive, and walk by faith, we return to the safety of the boat.

Nurture the divine nature within.

Ponder and Practice

Congratulations! I am so proud of you for completing this book and the healthy routines you have adopted. Take time to answer these important final questions to measure your progress and then meet me in the conclusion for some closing thoughts and a way to keep in touch.

According to our focal verse, what do we possess?

_____

_____

_____

What does it mean to know Jesus?

_____

_____

_____

Read the questions and your answers from Days 3 and 4. What changes have occurred since then?

_____

_____

_____

_____

_____

In what ways has your understanding of the armor of God and how to dress in it changed your life?

_____

_____

_____

Are you using the three Rs? How has that helped you?

_____

_____

_____

What spiritual growth and transformations have you experienced in the past sixty days?

_____

_____

_____

Our enemy seeks to destroy our new habits. Are you prepared to fight? What is your battle plan?

_____

_____

_____

Prayer

Jesus, I thank You for the faith that encourages me to live the abundant life, walking with You on the water of life. Continue to help me dress in the armor daily, replace the lies with truth, and walk all over my storms. In Jesus's name. Amen.

CONCLUSION

YOU MADE IT! YOU HAVE BROKEN FREE FROM THE PRISON BARS OF emotional bondage. Fear no longer freezes you. You know how to replace worry with worship and exchange panic for peace. You can stop the stress of life, and you have a bold, new faith.

Treat yourself to something nice. You have done a lot of hard work, and you deserve it.

But the work is never done. You have an angry enemy, and he isn't going to leave you alone because you've declared victory. Keep up the hard work of dressing in the armor of God. Continue using the three Rs (reveal the lie, remove the lie, and replace it with God's truth).

Keep this book handy like a toolbox. Dog-ear some pages, use bookmarks, and remember your favorite sections. You will need to refer to it occasionally because we still live in the flesh, and our feelings still want to boss us around.

I will continue to pray for you, and I'd really love to connect with you. Here's how we can do that.

Join my Facebook group, A Mountain of Faith Women's Ministry: https://www.facebook.com/groups/140942697610835/

Beginning January 2023, tune in to my YouTube channel for my new show, The Walk on Water Show, for encouragement. You'll find the link below.

Visit me at my website, where you can subscribe to my email list for some free gifts: www.amountainoffaith.com

Join me on social media:

- Email: amountainoffaith@gmail.com

- Facebook: https://m.facebook.com/carolyndalenewell/
- YouTube: https://www.youtube.com/channel/
  UC126VS7qlK8MFwJgdyiqCQQ
- LinkedIn: http://www.linkedin.com/in/carolyndnewell/en
- Instagram: https://www.instagram.com/carolyn.newell.142

More Books by Carolyn

Eyes of Faith: Winning the Battle Between Our Feelings and Our Faith

Overcoming the Overwhelming: Walking in Victorious Faith When You Don't Feel Victorious

Faith, Freedom, and 4 Paws: Seeing God Through Iva's Eyes (Guide Dog Tales Book 1)

Walking by Faith, Not Sight: 30 Inspirational Moments with Iva (Guide Dog Tales Book 2)

About the Author

CHRISTIAN SPEAKER AND AUTHOR CAROLYN DALE NEWELL EQUIPS women to break free from emotional strongholds and live transformed lives. She has authored seven books including her Guide Dog Tales devotional series and *Faith that Walks on Water*, a devotional journal. Carolyn loves digging deep into Scripture and discovering truths to share with her readers.

She is currently enrolled at the Tony Evans Training Center, where she has earned a certificate in Biblical and Theological Foundations. She is a contributor for iBelieve.com and Arise Daily. Carolyn is a member of the Advanced Writers and Speakers Association (AWSA) and a certified AWSA P.O.W.E.R. speaker.

Carolyn lives with blindness, but she calls her disability a gift from God. Carolyn resides in the Blue Ridge Mountains of Virginia with her husband, Tim. She loves reading, pizza, and discovering new independence with Iva, her guide dog.

Appendix A

10 Bible Truths in a Hurry

1. Be strong and of good courage, do not fear nor be afraid of them; for the Lord your God, He is the One who goes with you. He will not leave you nor forsake you. (Deuteronomy 31:6)
2. The fear of man brings a snare, but whoever trusts in the Lord shall be safe. (Proverbs 29:25)
3. "No weapon formed against you shall prosper, And every tongue which rises against you in judgment You shall condemn. This is the heritage of the servants of the Lord, And their righteousness is from Me," says the Lord. (Isaiah 54:17)
4. The thief does not come except to steal, and to kill, and to destroy. I have come that they may have life, and that they may have it more abundantly. (John 10:10)
5. For God has not given us a spirit of fear, but of power and of love and of a sound mind. (2 Timothy 1:7)
6. Put on the whole armor of God, that you may be able to stand against the wiles of the devil. For we do not wrestle against flesh and blood, but against principalities, against powers, against the rulers of the darkness of this age, against spiritual hosts of wickedness in the heavenly places. (Ephesians 6:11–12)
7. You will keep him in perfect peace, whose mind is stayed on You, because he trusts in You. (Isaiah 26:3)
8. He gives power to the weak, and to those who have no might He increases strength. (Isaiah 40:29)

9. You are of God, little children, and have overcome them, because He who is in you is greater than he who is in the world. (1 John 4:4)
10. For the word of God is living and powerful, and sharper than any two-edged sword, piercing even to the division of soul and spirit, and of joints and marrow, and is a discerner of the thoughts and intents of the heart. (Hebrews 4:12)

Endnotes

1. Tony Evans, *Kingdom Heroes: Building a Strong Faith That Endures* (Eugene, Oregon: Harvest House Publishers, 2021) chapter 1 Kindle.

2. Tony Evans, *Tony Evans Bible Commentary* (Nashville: Holman Bible Publishers, 2019), 1 Corinthians 1:18, Kindle.

3. James Strong, *Strong's Expanded Exhaustive Concordance of the Bible* (Nashville: Thomas Nelson), https://biblehub.com/strongs/1_samuel/17-28.htm.

4. Tony Evans, *The Fire That Ignites: Living in the Power of the Holy Spirit,* Life Change Books (New York: Penguin Random House, 2008), chapter 3, Kindle.

5. "Anorexia Facts & Statistics," Eating Recovery Center, accessed August 20, 2022, https://www.eatingrecoverycenter.com/conditions/anorexia/facts-statistics

6. Tony Evans, *Life Essentials for Knowing God Better, Experiencing God Deeper, Loving God More* (Chicago: Moody Publishers, 2003), chapter 8, Kindle.

7. Warren W. Wiersbe, *Be Confident (Hebrews): Live by Faith, Not by Sight,* The BE Bible Study Series (Colorado Springs: David C. Cook, 2009), chapter 5, Kindle.

8. Warren W. Wiersbe, The BE Bible Study Series (Colorado Springs, CO: David C. Cook, 2009), https://www.biblegateway.com/passage/?search=john+15%3A13&version=NKJV.

9. Lysa TerKeurst, *Uninvited: Living Loved When You Feel Less Than, Left Out, and Lonely* (Nashville: Nelson Books, 2016), chapter 4, Kindle.

10. Shannon Popkin, *Comparison Girl: Lessons from Jesus on Me-Free Living in a Measure-Up World* (Grand Rapids, MI: Kregel Publications, 2020), Introduction, Kindle.

11. Warren W. Weirsbe, *Be Courageous (Luke 14–24): Take Heart from Christ's Example,* The BE Bible Study Series (Colorado Springs, CO: David C. Cook, 2010), chapter 9, Kindle.

12. Nicki Koziarz, *Why Her? 6 Truths We Need to Hear When Measuring Up Leaves Us Falling Behind* (Nashville: B&H Books, 2018), chapter 10, Kindle.

13. Minesh Kahtri, MD, reviewer, "How Worry Affects Your Body," WebMD, August 22, 2021, https://www.webmd.com/anxiety-panic/ss/slideshow-worry-body-effects.

14. Warren W. Wiersbe, *Be Compassionate (Luke 1–13): Let the World Know That Jesus Cares*, The BE Bible Study Series (Colorado Springs, CO: David C. Cook, 1988), chapter 9, Kindle.

15. Warren W. Wiersbe, *Be Compassionate (Luke 1–13): Let the World Know That Jesus Cares*, The BE Bible Study Series (Colorado Springs, CO: David C. Cook, 1988), chapter 9, Kindle.

16. Phillip W. Keller, *A Shepherd Looks at Psalm 23* (Grand Rapids, MI: Zondervan, 1970, 2007, 2015), chapters 3 and 4, Kindle.

17. Phillip W. Keller, *A Shepherd Looks at Psalm 23* (Grand Rapids, MI: Zondervan, 2015), chapters 3 and 4, Kindle.

18. Liz Curtis Higgs, *The Girl's Still Got It* (Colorado Springs: Waterbrook Press, 2012), chapter 4, Kindle.

19. John MacArthur, *NKJV MacArthur Study Bible* (Nashville: Word Publishing, 1997), Matthew 18:24, Kindle.

20. Corrie ten Boom, "Guideposts Classics: Corrie ten Boom on Forgiveness," *Guideposts*, (November, 1972), https://www.guideposts.org/better-living/positive-living/guideposts-classics-corrie-ten-boom-forgiveness.

21. Warren W. Wiersbe, *Be Exultant (Psalms 90–150): Praising God for His Mighty Works,* The BE Bible Study Series (Colorado Springs, CO: David C. Cook, 2004), chapter 2, Kindle.

22. James Strong, *Strong's Expanded Exhaustive Concordance of the Bible.* https://biblehub.com/strongs/psalms/42-5.htm

23. Phillip W. Keller, *A Shepherd Looks at Psalm 23* (Grand Rapids, MI: Zondervan, 2015), chapter 5, Kindle.

24. Phillip W. Keller, *A Shepherd Looks at Psalm 23* (Grand Rapids, MI: Zondervan, 2015), chapter 5, Kindle.

25. Warren W. Wiersbe, *Be Worshipful (Psalms 1–89): Glorifying God for Who He Is,* The BE Bible Study Series (Colorado Springs, CO: David C. Cook, 2004), chapter 1, Kindle.

26. Warren W. Wiersbe, *Be Alert (2 Peter, 2&3 John, Jude): Beware of the Religious Impostors,* The BE Bible Study Series (Colorado Springs, CO: David C. Cook, 2010), chapter 1, Kindle.

27. Warren W. Wiersbe, *Be Alert (2 Peter, 2&3 John, Jude): Beware of the Religious Impostors,* The BE Bible Study Series (Colorado Springs, CO: David C. Cook, 2010). chapter 1, Kindle.

28. Tony Evans, *Tony Evans Bible Commentary* (Nashville: Holman Bible Publishers, 2019), 2 Peter 1:3, Kindle.

ORDER INFORMATION

REDEMPTION
P R E S S

To order additional copies of this book, please visit
www.redemption-press.com.
Also available at Amazon, Christian bookstores,
and Barnes and Noble.